Defining Moments

Defining Moments

Memorable and Inspiring Stories
from Outstanding Leaders

Bill and Phyllis Nichols, Editors

Defining Moments: Memorable and Inspiring Stories from Outstanding Leaders

Published by GWN Publishing

ISBN: 978-1-7369157-8-3 (paperback)
ISBN: 978-1-7369157-9-0 (ebook)

CONTENTS

Introduction	vii
Jim Adams	1
William W. (Bill) Airy	11
Gretchen Berggren, MD	21
Ruth E. Berggren, MD	31
Chris Buckingham	43
Dr. Ricky Burk	55
Rachael M. Colby	67
Jackie K. Cooper	81
Letha Cole Crouch	91
Yudith Cavazos Cruz	101
Dr. Jim Denison	113
Dr. Dean Dickens	123
Karr La Dickens	135
Linda Hibner	147
Dr. Dale E. Klein	159
Rebecca A. Klein	167
Dr. Adena Williams Loston	177

Dr. Nora O. Lozano	185
Norvi Maribel Mayfield	195
Merlin Merritt	209
Andy Muck, MD	221
Dr. Frank Newport	233
Jan Evans Patterson, MD	243
Dr. Jack Robbins	255
Camille Bishop Simmons	265
Dr. Larry Williams	277
Dr. George W. (Bill) Nichols	285
Phyllis Clark Nichols	297

Introduction

From Bill:

My wife, Phyllis, and I are writers in this season of our lives. She is a novelist and a devotional writer, while I write about theological issues, biblical studies, and discipleship. We both know and appreciate the power of the story.

A while back in my morning devotional time, I came across a scripture that spoke to me as it never had before. Simon Peter wrote to his friends, "Make sure you always remember these things after I'm gone" (2 Peter 1:15 NLT). That verse initiated conversation with Phyllis about the few special "things" or what we call *defining moments* in our lives—those unforgettable experiences that made a significant impact on our lives and our work and were certainly spiritual lessons that we never forgot. I'm sure you can remember some of those times in your past.

Mark Batterson in his book *Soul Print* says that each of us experiences millions of events that are recorded in our brains. Research indicates we remember less than one percent of those events. And only one percent of that one percent of memories become defining moments. Those are the times that we never forget. They shape our beliefs, values, and goals in life, and sometimes they can be so powerful that they change even the trajectory of our lives.

Over the years as a teacher and preacher, I have learned the importance of reading, writing, and telling stories to teach great spiritual truths. Jim Loehr, *New York Times* bestselling author and leader of the Human Performance Institute, said, "Our capacity to tell stories is one of our profoundest gifts." Mark Sanborn, popular motivational speaker and bestselling author, said, "Stories are the effective communicator's most powerful tool." We all know the power of a story told well.

As I meditated on this verse from 2 Peter, I also remembered Jesus and the apostle Paul. Whether it was when the multitudes gathered around Him or in an intimate setting with His disciples, Jesus taught most of His truths through simple, relatable, and memorable stories—telling parables rather than teaching platitudes. None of us could forget the story of the Prodigal Son or the Good Samaritan and the lessons we learn from these stories. And then we see Paul retelling to anyone who would listen the story of His encounter with Christ on the road to Damascus—that defining moment that transformed not only his life and but changed the course of human history.

We have been blessed through our lives with such interesting friends who are committed to a life of faith no matter their vocation. With all these thoughts in mind, the idea came to ask some of our friends from various backgrounds to remember such defining moments in their lives, to write them down, and to allow us to compile these stories into a book—the kind of book that would be impactful, encouraging, comforting, and inspirational. We invited twenty-six of those friends to partner with us to bring you this book. They come from different career backgrounds, yet they are deeply spiritual men and women who are walking-around libraries.

Some of them shared childhood memories, and others shared events that happened later in their lives. For some it was an experience with a family member, friend, teacher, or mentor who made a significant difference in their lives. Some of their defining moments were painful or difficult, while others were happy experiences. We hope you will enjoy the stories of their defining moments.

While this book took a great deal of time and effort on the part of many, we have partnered together to give all proceeds of the sales of this book to Samaritan's Purse, a ministry of the Billy Graham Evangelistic Association, for relief efforts around the world, especially the immediate needs in Ukraine, which will be ongoing for years. We thank you for partnering with us by purchasing this book. We pray you will be blessed as you read these stories, and we hope you feel as we do: blessed to give so that others can go where we cannot and give help and hope in Jesus' name.

From Phyllis:

There are many characters who walk in and out of our life stories. Some of those characters, like our parents and siblings and children, God chose for us. And then God in His goodness allows us to choose some of those characters for ourselves—our friends. Bill and I have agreed that we think God chose our friends for us, too, for they have been and are such marvelous gifts to us.

These friends who share their defining moments in this book are people with whom we have done life. We could write volumes about our own experiences with these good folks. We have worked, played, prayed, served, traveled, laughed, and cried with them. Whether we were in the office, on a church pew, around the piano, in the boardroom, in a cinderblock church in the middle of a Guatemalan cornfield, on a cruise ship, a hospital room, or around our table, we have shared so many moments and the meaningful things of life with these good and godly people.

It has been amazing to see all the different settings, circumstances, and times in their lives when their defining moments occurred. You will read about faraway places such as Congo, India, the Philippines, Honduras, Haiti, and even outer space. You'll meet parents, teachers, and preachers who created defining moments in the lives of these. And then you'll read about hospital scenes, the battlefield, and those moments of solitude in quiet places where God made Himself known.

As we began to compile these stories, we noticed there was one golden thread woven through each one: that golden thread of God's presence and His activity in their lives no matter the setting. We are so grateful their stories and our stories and God's story are woven together in love forever.

Another obvious truth became apparent. Their defining moments had ripple effects. Like tossing a pebble in a pool, the ripples cannot be stopped. Sometimes those ripples impacted not only the lives of the storytellers themselves but rippled through the lives of others too. That's how God often works.

When Bill and I began to talk about the book cover, we thought of an ancient clock tower symbolizing the time and the moments of our days. But somehow, after reading the stories of these defining moments, the image of that pebble's contact with the surface of the water kept returning, and the book cover appeared under Bill's skillful eye and hands. Just ponder the significance of the ripples you make and the ripples of others on your life.

When we invited our friends to partner with us, we asked them to imagine sitting on the front porch with a friend and telling their stories. We also explained that their stories would not be professionally edited because we wanted their stories to have their voices, their personalities, and their passions. You will experience this as you read their biographical sketches and see their photos and then read their stories.

What a serendipitous blessing it has been to work on this project and to know that our friends' stories will bless lives and that the proceeds from book sales will also bless lives. We have enjoyed every interaction, the recall of our own memories with each of these, and the sheer delight in the of reading their stories.

Our prayer is that these stories of defining moments will resonate with you and will encourage you to recall some defining moments in your life. Thank God for those moments, and perhaps you need to acknowledge someone else too. And we hope this book will be an encouragement to you to share your own defining moments whether in conversation with a friend or writing them down as a legacy for your family so that, as Peter said, they'll remember these things after you're gone.

Bill and Phyllis Nichols

Jim Adams

A NATIVE OF San Antonio, TX, Jim received his BS from Texas A&M University and his MBA from the University of Texas. He was president and CEO of Southwestern Bell and subsequently chairman of Texas Instruments. In addition to a number of corporate boards, he has served on the boards of Baylor University, Baylor Health System, University Health System in San Antonio, Raise your Hand Texas, and P16 Council of Bexar County and was cofounder of Communities in Schools in Texas. Jim was chairman of the board of directors of Oncor Electric Delivery.

Jim also served on the advisory board of the Hankamer School of Business at Baylor, the engineering advisory board of the University of Texas and the

College of Science board at Texas A&M.

His passion is education. Jim is president of a scholarship foundation that provides scholarships in his alma mater school district of Harlandale ISD in San Antonio. All seniors from this school district who continue their education receive a scholarship.

Jim and his wife, Judy, have three children and reside in San Antonio, Texas, where they are very involved in Trinity Baptist Church.

From the Back Row to a Bugle Call

A defining moment does not always come as a flash. Sometimes moments accumulate until we come to an understanding that perhaps God was using those events, those relationships, or those experiences to shape our lives. I had such a series of moments as a high-school student at Harlandale High School in San Antonio, TX.

I was discovering girls, but I admit, for me, understanding math and physics was easier than understanding girls. I was a good and responsible student, but I was shy and tended to sit in the back of the classroom. So, I was quite amazed when Mrs. Mullins, my homeroom teacher who was also the speech and drama teacher, chose me for a role in the stage play *A Date with Judy*. My explanation of being disinterested fell on deaf ears. It seems that Mrs. Mullins was determined to cast me as Randolph, a teenager who was always in trouble. I can assure you I was not typecast.

Rehearsals began, and my resentment and reluctance waned as I began to enjoy the rehearsals. Through this experience, I discovered I was somewhat of a ham. In dress rehearsal, I put my whole self into that role, and I actually became a showstopper on the opening night. *A Date with Judy* was indeed a success, and I found it much easier to get dates after my showstopping performance.

The next year, when it came time for the annual production, Mrs. Mullins came to me again. She was casting me in a particular role in *Arsenic and Old Lace*. Once again, my explanation of disinterest and my lack of time for such an activity fell on deaf ears. Her response was, "Just make time, James." So, I found myself playing the role of Teddy Brewster, a likable and kindhearted middle-aged man who believed he was Teddy Roosevelt. I was playing the role of a character who was enacting a role himself. It was quite a physical role, as Teddy had to dash up the stairs yelling, "Charge!" and playing his trumpet. Over the weeks of rehearsal, I grew bolder in taking on this character. I played this role with such fervor that I was voted the Male Dramatist of the Year.

Fifty years later, Judy and I attended my fiftieth high school reunion. I was introduced as James Adams, the guy with a trumpet who stole the show in *Arsenic and Old Lace*. That remembrance was such a surprise because I still see myself sitting on the back row.

Looking back, I think I would not have chosen those experiences for myself, but Mrs. Mullins chose them for me and nudged me into those roles. I had no notion as a shy sophomore that my career would require considerable public speaking, sometimes in front of thousands of people. These experiences gave me a different sense of myself. I was no longer the shy young man on the back row. My fear and reluctance were things of the past. Mrs. Mullins had led me to opportunities where I learned those valuable lessons on a stage in a high school in San

Antonio, TX. I now understand those experiences as some defining moments.

As time passed, my mother maintained a relationship with Mrs. Mullins. You might imagine that through the years of teaching and investing in other students like me, Mrs. Mullins was greatly loved. When our company relocated from St. Louis, MO, to San Antonio, TX, I took an opportunity to visit Mrs. Mullins. What a joy it was to see her and relive some of those memories. And what a blessing it was to hear her say, "James, I always thought you'd make something of yourself."

Mrs. Mullins was a wise woman, but she was not entirely right. There were many who invested in me, and then I had a gracious God to guide my path. I did not make something of myself all by myself.

As a follower of Christ, I do not believe in coincidences. It was no coincidence that I was given these high school experiences to draw me from the back row. Mrs. Mullins saw something in me, and I believe God used her to prepare me for what He knew was ahead.

The Bible is filled with real men and women who were prepared for their life purposes in ways they would not have chosen for themselves. Look at Moses as his story begins in the book of Exodus and continues through Leviticus and Numbers and ends in Deuteronomy. His start as a baby in the bulrushes, found and adopted by the pharaoh's daughter, was probably not a start he would have chosen. But God orchestrated that his mother would teach him about his people and their God. Then God orchestrated Moses' palace education, all these experiences preparing him to lead his people out of the bondage of Egypt and into the land God had prepared for them.

Think of Esther, a poor young Jewish girl, who through events that only God could have ordained, became Queen Esther. Her faithful uncle was instrumental in preparing her for her toughest assignment. She found herself in a position and summoned up her bravery and saved her people from annihilation. God had a plan and a purpose for her, and He prepared her for it.

Look at Timothy sitting at the feet of his mother and grandmother. Lois and Eunice are powerful examples of the impact a godly mother and grandmother can have on the life of a young man. Their teaching prepared young Timothy to be Paul's companion, scribe, and disciple. Timothy played a critical role in the spread of the gospel. God did not leave Timothy's upbringing and preparation to chance.

I am no Moses, Esther, or Timothy. I am an ordinary man, a sitting-on-the-back-row kind of guy, who had the great blessings of good parents and teachers, especially Mrs. Mullins. They invested themselves in me, and I see now how they were used by my heavenly Father to prepare me for life and responsibilities I would be given. I believe that He directed my steps, my every step. As King Solomon, the wisest man who ever lived, said, "We can make our plans, but the LORD determines our steps" (Proverbs 16:9 NLT).

A Ring of Truth

One question stopped me in my steps: a question that was designed and pointed at me at just the right time. I have vivid memories of exactly where I was when that question was asked of me. It was truly a defining moment.

As a young college graduate about to launch out in the world, I had no interest in working for a large company. But God directed my steps, and I became employed by Southwestern Bell, an AT&T company. They were huge, and they were into computers, which was the new technology of the day.

I found myself literally working over a hundred hours a week. We were just learning of the far-reaching and expansive capabilities computers had. There was far more data than we could input inside normal work weeks. I would literally set up the computer to run, and I would nap until the clicking stopped, and then I could start the next round.

For more than a year, I worked day and night without feedback from management. There were times I felt like a miner, down in a dark hole, grinding and chipping away, and no one was seeing what I was doing. I seemed to be void of light. After this year without feedback, I was sent to Houston to take some computer courses. Before I went, I was told to visit Mr. Doyle Rogers.

Mr. Doyle Rogers was the general manager for South Texas and was several levels above me in management. He accepted my request for a meeting and received me into his office. For someone who felt like he had lived alone in a dungeon of work for over a year, I found myself in the largest office I had ever seen, like I had been ushered into the throne room of a king. He invited me to sit down, and thus began a conversation that guided my future career.

Mr. Doyle said, "James, I hear that you're a fine employee. In fact, I heard that you can do the work of one and a half people." I thanked him for the compliment and told him I hoped it was true.

He then added, "Some seem to think you actually do the work of two or more people."

I responded, "Sir, I thank you, but that may be pushing it." I'm not exactly sure what I expected, but this meeting was not going as I had anticipated. It seemed he was taking my "corporate temperature."

Quietly pausing, Mr. Rogers leaned over his desk and peered at me. Then came *the* question. "James, have you ever stopped to think how much you could get done if you didn't feel you had to do it all yourself? Have you thought of what might happen if you delegated some of this work to your staff and colleagues?"

There are some words that you hear on occasion that just have that ring of truth. That question had a real ring of truth and has never been lost from me. I was ready to hear it, and I listened. It jolted me in a way that changed the way I worked. In fact, over the next several years, Mr. Rogers promoted me three or four times before he left the company, and I was chosen to take his position.

Over the decades, I enjoyed working for a company that valued integrity, ethics, and opportunities for growth and training for its employees. Because I had been given opportunities for good and meaningful work, I wanted to do the same for others out of my gratitude. I became a delegator, working hard to give others responsibility and providing them fertile ground where they could grow as persons and employees. I learned from mentors and good leaders before me that leadership has to do with surrounding yourself with good people who will share the responsibilities and opportunities. I was blessed again to be surrounded by good and hardworking people. I was also known for providing an environment where women could advance. I believe these to be biblical principles. All of this because of how God spoke to me through *the* question Mr. Rogers asked me.

I still maintain a friendly relationship with Mr. Doyle Rogers, now ninety-five years of age. We enjoy sitting around talking about the wonderful work opportunities given to a couple of ordinary guys.

Although I had tremendous respect for him when he asked me *the* question all those years ago, I realize the question he asked came from a higher place than from behind his desk. It seemed to me that those words came from God Himself through the voice of Mr. Rogers. They came at a time when I could hear them and at a time when I needed them. They shaped my work life.

I look at my Lord Jesus. He came to earth for a purpose. The first thing He did when beginning His public ministry was to call others to help Him. He knew that soon He would no longer be on the earth and that others would have to carry on His mission in spreading Truth and Light.

It was an odd group of twelve men, from fishermen to a tax collector—ordinary men chosen and equipped by Jesus Himself to do an extraordinary mission. What Jesus did and what those men continued to do after Jesus completed His work on earth changed the world and human history forever. Jesus called these men and gave them an opportunity to live out their purposes.

I'm like the fisherman—just a plain, ordinary, vanilla kind of guy—but I had the blessing of a number of good jobs, jobs that gave me opportunity to provide opportunities for others.

The apostle Paul admonishes us, "Let us think of ways to motivate one another to acts of love and good works" (Hebrews 10:24 NLT). Others motivated me, and it is my responsibility to motivate others to be the best they can be. Truly that is a worthy purpose and ambition.

William W. (Bill) Airy

William W. (Bill) Airy was born and grew up in Albuquerque, NM. He graduated cum laude from Fort Lewis College in Durango, CO, in 1976 and received his master of international management degree from Thunderbird Graduate School in Glendale, AZ, in 1977.

Bill had a long career in the film and television industries in Denver, Los Angeles, and Charlotte, NC. He was a senior executive at Tele-Communications, Inc., and Liberty Media Corporation in Denver, CO, for seventeen years. While at Liberty Media, he developed the cable television network that ultimately became the Hallmark Channel. He also helped to launch a Liberty Media-owned film and television content management and distribution company called Ascent Media, which was based in Los Angeles with operations in LA, New York, London, and Singapore. In 2005 Bill left the secular media world and joined Inspiration Networks in Charlotte, NC, as the chief operating officer. He subsequently joined LeSEA Broadcasting in South Bend, IN, as the chief strategy officer.

Now retired, Bill holds real-estate licenses in both Colorado and New Mexico and together with his wife, Linda, invests in and manages real-estate properties in various states. In the past, Bill has also volunteered with the Gideon's organization placing bibles in hotel rooms, prisons, and military induction centers.

Bill and his wife, Linda, raised five children in New Mexico and Colorado and are now the proud grandparents of fifteen grandchildren. To be near family, they currently have homes in Gulf Breeze, FL, and Albuquerque, NM. Bill and his wife are members of the Mission Anglican Church in Pensacola, FL. But most of all, he enjoys spending time with friends and family in Florida, New Mexico, North Carolina, and Colorado.

Have you ever heard God speaking to you? I mean really speaking to you. With a voice. It has happened only three times to me in my sixty-eight years. The stories I am about to tell are true and are shared with the hope that they may help others who have struggled with some of the things I have struggled with in my life.

Meeting Jesus

As a young boy growing up in Albuquerque, New Mexico, I watched the moms and dads in our neighborhood, many of whom had survived horrific things in Europe, Africa, Southeast Asia, and the South Pacific during World War II, as they attempted to deal with their demons by consuming copious amounts of alcohol on a daily basis. Alcohol was everywhere in our neighborhood, and my friends and I took advantage of its availability, and we started drinking secretly while we were in our preteen years.

In the late sixties, my buddies and I were entering high school. At that time drugs had taken the place of alcohol, and the counterculture lifestyle permeated our high school campus. I took a deep dive into this world and got involved in things I never should have experienced. My parents ultimately discovered what I was doing, and they were clearly shocked and hurt. My older brother and sister had already gone off to college, and both of them were having stellar collegiate careers. So, my failings were particularly painful for my parents.

It was during this time that I was invited by one of our high school cheerleaders (whose name was Valerie) to go with her to a Christian coffeehouse called The Way that had recently opened in a newer part of town. It was part of what later would become known as the Jesus Movement. The Way featured big beanbag chairs, upbeat music from contemporary Christian artists like Keith Green and many others, good coffee, and good people. Several of these young Christians, together with Valerie, the girl who had invited me, started telling me about Jesus. I knew at the time that my parents were Christians. My dad read the Bible regularly, and I know he prayed nearly every evening, but our family seldom went to church together. It just wasn't something we did.

But something about what I was hearing that night hit home. When Valerie asked me if I wanted to accept Jesus into my life, I said yes. Word got around quickly at The Way, and there was yelling and clapping and lots of hugs and smiles. In my heart, in my mind, I heard a voice that said, "Follow Me." That was the first time I think I heard God's voice.

I was filled with excitement and joy. The next day I went to some of my buddies and told them my good news. I just knew they, too, would want to join me in this wonderful new relationship with Jesus. Uh, not so much. If anything, my enthusiasm was perceived as a better-than-thou attitude, and they wanted to have nothing to do with me or my Jesus. I persisted, they resisted.

And so it went. We graduated, I went off to college, played football, backslid somewhat, but always tried to maintain my Christian witness with anyone who would listen.

Meeting My Wife

AFTER COLLEGE AND graduate school, I went back to Albuquerque to work in our family business, an advertising agency. By this time, I had backslidden pretty badly. I was working at the ad agency during the day, and at night I worked as a bouncer at a biker bar on Central Avenue in Albuquerque, the old Route 66. I was burning the candle at both ends, getting into fights almost every night, and drinking heavily.

One day I was having lunch with a client of the ad agency and a lovely young lady was our waitress. She told us her name was Linda. I mentioned to my client, whose name was Joe, that I thought Linda was cute. When she came back to our table, Joe said, "My friend here thinks you are cute, but he is too shy to ask you for a date. Would you consider giving him your phone number so he can give you a call?"

I was mortified. I stumbled around for something to say, and I think I muttered something about wondering how long she had been working at the restaurant. She responded and said that it was just a temporary job, that she had applied for a job at Christian Center's daycare facility. Christian Center was Albuquerque's first megachurch and was well known throughout the community.

At that precise moment, I heard a voice say to me, "This is the woman I want you to marry." I looked around to see if anyone else had heard the voice. Joe and Linda were just looking at me, waiting for me to respond to her answer to my question. I think I probably muttered something like, "Oh, that's nice," or something to that effect.

But to my amazement, Linda wrote her phone number on a slip of paper and gave it to me. I called her and asked her out. Our first date didn't go well. I had initially taken her to a rock concert and a big fight broke out. She wanted to leave, and so I took her to a bar. Again, not a great choice if you are trying to impress a Christian girl. I realized things were going badly, and at one point I needed to get some cash from an ATM. As I was leaving I said to her, "I'll be right back, unless the Rapture happens first!"

Clumsy, without a doubt. But it worked. When I got back, she was smiling, and she asked, somewhat incredulously, "Are you a Christian?"

I replied, "Yes, I am!"

And we had a nice conversation after that. She told me that she had previously been married and that her first husband had died. She had two daughters; the oldest was three and the youngest was nine months. What was resonating in my head was the voice that had said to me, "This is the woman I want you to marry." During that dinner, I asked Linda to marry me. She said, "Yes," and three months later we were married.

That was forty-four years ago. We now have five

children, all married, all believers, and fifteen grandchildren. And they are all believers as well.

Thank you, Jesus, for speaking to me when I needed to hear Your voice. I will be eternally grateful.

Transformation

After marriage, my career took off. I entered the cable television business and had the great good fortune to work for a true visionary—Dr. John Malone—at Tele-Communications, Inc., and subsequently at Liberty Media Corporation. I was there for a total of seventeen years. There were many great experiences and many wonderful relationships that have endured, one of which was with Dr. Bill Nichols and his wonderful wife, Phyllis.

What most of my friends and family didn't know is that during most of my adult life, I was a functional alcoholic. I drank alone, never before work, and I was able to hide it pretty well. Linda knew that I drank occasionally, but she didn't know how often and how much. I fought the demon of alcohol addiction every day for thirty years. I would quit for one, two, or three weeks only to slide back into daily consumption every time I had quit.

After I left working for Liberty Media, I worked for two Christian cable television network ministries. At one of those jobs, I met a pastor named Myles Munroe. Myles spoke to me about the Kingdom of God. He said the Kingdom of God is why Jesus came to live among us. His words triggered something inside of me. I wanted to know more. He said that Jesus had given Peter the keys to the Kingdom of God and that with those keys the doors I unlocked on earth would be unlocked in heaven. And the doors I locked on earth would be locked in heaven.

One day, as I was coming home from work to pour myself a large rum and coke, my drink of preference, I was entering our driveway and I was meditating on Matthew 16:19. I remember saying, "Father, I am locking this door of alcohol on earth, and I'm asking you to lock it in heaven." At that instant I heard a voice say to me, "Throw it away. You don't need it anymore." I had a physical sensation of a weight being lifted off my shoulders.

I went into the house, gathered up all the rum bottles I had hidden around in various places and poured them down the kitchen sink. When Linda got home, I confessed everything to her and told her what had just happened to me on the driveway with the voice and inside the house with the rum bottles and the kitchen sink. There was, of course, initially some skepticism on her part, but I haven't had a drink of alcohol since that day. The *desire* for alcoholic drink had left me completely. The date was January 15, 2013.

That was the third time I heard God's voice. And again, I will be eternally grateful for what He said to me that day.

Gretchen Berggren, MD

BORN IN CHADRON, Nebraska, Gretchen Glode Berggren became the only female member of the class of 1958 at the University of Nebraska College of Medicine. She went on to study at the Belgian Institute of Tropical Medicine and Hygiene before joining her husband, Dr. Warren Berggren, at the Institut Medical Evangelique in Congo. They led Congolese nurse trainees to become highly skilled medical assistants.

Following Congo's political independence, Dr. Berggren served in the Ubangi District and helped found the Congo Protestant Relief Agency, which brought in over 250 American and European physicians to fill gaps left by fleeing Belgian personnel.

Dr. Berggren later trained at Harvard and became a

faculty member of the Harvard School of Public Health Department of Population Sciences. She joined her husband in field projects at the Hospital Albert Schweitzer in Deschapelles, Haiti, where she served and trained Harvard medical and public health students. Simultaneously, they were raising their two daughters: Dr. Ruth Berggren and Carol Jeanne Tanski.

She was honored at the White House by President Clinton and UNICEF for her role in reducing child mortality rates and later, along with her husband, was with presented an award by the hands of Mother Teresa at the National Council for International Health. Gretchen joined her husband in worldwide work with Save the Children, most recently concentrating on community-based methods to combat malnutrition.

Dr. Berggren presently resides in Colorado.

Lessons Learned and Insights from Celebrating the Lord's Supper with Congolese Christians

MY HUSBAND, DR. Warren Berggren, and I arrived in 1959 at Institute Medicals Evangelique (IME) near Kinshasa (Leopoldville), a teaching hospital to train Congolese nurses, both male and female. With completed training as physicians in the United States, we had studied in Antwerp with other medical missionaries, both Catholic and Protestant, from Europe, the USA, and Canada. Pastors from many denominations were part of the teaching team that Warren was asked to direct.

Congolese students spoke many languages, but all were fluent in French and could follow the curriculum developed not only to train them in nursing but also as medical and surgical technicians destined to serve in far-flung clinics. Little did we know at the time that a few years later, when over five hundred medical workers would flee the Congo during a revolution for independence, our students would use their skills to save hundreds of lives.

Patients from many different tribal backgrounds descended daily on the hospital. They were suffering from tropical diseases such as malaria and snail fever and from leprosy, tuberculosis, wounds from hunting accidents, and needs for surgical interventions. Many of their families set up camp on nearby riverbanks in order to help attend to the hospitalized family members. This made for a busy atmosphere along the periphery of the hospital grounds where the smell of cooking fires was pervasive. Women washed their clothing on the riverbanks.

We learned that at a church on the compound there would be native pastors from different denominations in charge of the services on Sundays. We also learned that once we were invited to participate, we would be welcome to participate in the Lord's Supper or communion at one of the Sabbath services.

This Sunday worship service was a busy scene—many languages, mostly French hymns, and much activity around families where mothers might be breastfeeding and often admonishing their other children to be quiet. We recognized the melodies in some of the songs, and we followed the sermon with our Bibles opened to the designated scripture.

The pastor emphasized the verses from Paul's first letter to the Corinthians:

> So anyone who eats this bread or drinks this cup of the Lord unworthily is guilty of sinning against the body and blood of the Lord. That is why you should examine yourself before eating the bread and drinking the cup. For if you eat the bread or drink the cup without honoring the body of Christ, you are eating and drinking God's judg-

> ment upon yourself. That is why many of you are weak and sick and some have even died. But if we would examine ourselves, we would not be judged by God in this way. (1 Corinthians 11:27–31 NLT)

We realized that the time had come for the observance of the Lord's Supper. The communion bread plates were carefully displayed and covered, and small glasses held whatever kind of juice might substitute for the wine. But then came a surprise: the pastor re-read the scripture from 1 Corinthians and quietly suggested that everyone go outside the church and communicate together. After the re-reading of the scripture, he spoke. As was interpreted for us, he said, "No, with family nearby, everyone should go outside and converse, asking forgiveness from any neighbor or family member if the Lord has laid it on your heart to do so. Then as you are led of the Lord, please come back into the church and take communion."

This announcement was followed by congregant action that was an even bigger surprise for us. Quietly, many rose and went outside the church before taking communion. We observed teenagers with tear-filled eyes approaching their mothers. Here and there a husband and wife quietly spoke to each other. Men were shaking each other's hands. And then some left the church, apparently to go home. Perhaps there was a need to ask forgiveness of someone else rather than taking the Lord's Supper unworthily.

Then with pastoral invitation, people began to reenter

the church, and the deacons of the church passed the communion bread and wine. Softly, the hymns were sung. There was a sense of utter peace and reverence. Our eyes filled with tears.

This was a turning point, a defining moment, in our understanding of the action needed in order not to take communion unworthily and to appreciate the reverence and preparation needed before partaking of the Lord's Supper. This moment was etched in our hearts, and we recalled it whenever we were privileged to participate in the Holy Eucharist.

The Timing of the Lord Is Perfect

IT WAS JUNE 1960. A Belgian pilot helped me up the steps into a small bush plane headed from the airport in Kinshasa, the new capital of the Congo, to a bush town called Libenge. The pilot looked puzzled.

In perfect French, the pilot asked, "Do you know where you are going, and I must ask, why are you going there?" Before I could answer, he pointed out, "You see, we have already unloaded the live chickens that our Congolese passengers tried to take on board. You may not know that livestock are not permitted on the bush planes even though the Congo is independent!"

I smiled, remembering that a hospitality gift in this country was often a chicken or a goat. "My husband is coming too," I said. "We are physicians from the Congo Protestant Relief Agency. There is a former Belgian government hospital in Libenge, and they have no doctors; the Congolese government asked us to come! We are coming to serve."

The pilot shook his head. "It is wild at Libenge. They are shooting elephants up there! When you land, you will see the tusks piled around the airport building. The natives still believe it is illegal to kill an elephant unless you give up the tusks to whoever is the government!"

I smiled and replied, "And I suppose you will tell me the rivers are full of crocodiles."

What I did not tell the pilot was that we were expecting our first baby, and that I was not only pregnant, but I was not feeling well. I was taking antimalarial medication, but the parasites had their way.

At last, my husband, Warren, climbed up the steps and into the bush airplane, his arms loaded with medical supplies. We began the rocky flight over jungle toward Libenge and the northern border.

Three Belgian nuns greeted us at the hospital, overjoyed that we were physicians, that we spoke French, and that they were no longer alone. Pilfering had become an art after independence, but these nuns had staunchly defended pharmaceutical supplies, a functional delivery room and surgical unit, and some lab supplies. The Congolese administrator had defended them and won their respect. After this welcome, we found buildings of a Protestant mission where we could abide.

Our pregnancy lasted nine months. I often felt the baby moving as I walked to work at the overcrowded pediatric clinic. Daily I listened to his tiny heart with my stethoscope. And then one morning there was no movement, no sound. I sent for Warren at the hospital, who rushed home to confirm my findings.

We felt very much alone. Our conversation was sad but as scientific as we could make it: "Would a C-section be appropriate? Was there anything more we could do? When would my labor start?"

And then we prayed, "Oh Lord, we are so alone; hear

us as we pray! Send us help!" And then I felt my labor contractions begin.

Unbeknownst to us, the Lord had awakened Dr. Gordon Johnson. With a sense of urgency in his heart, he was already on his way, driving as fast as he could over rutty roads and dangerous bridges from his mission hospital at Tandala to be beside us. We heard a car screeching from the driveway as Dr. Johnson arrived. Warren ran to meet him.

Dr. Johnson was not surprised at our sad news. "You should not be alone!" he said. "I am taking over."

He gently confirmed our findings and felt a C-section would be inappropriate. So, our baby boy was stillborn in the Congo. While his tiny casket was being built, Dr. Johnson examined the baby's heart.

"Several malformations incompatible with life," he concluded. And then, "I am staying with you for a while! Our Lord knew you should not be alone!"

How often, as I remember this, I am reminded that the Lord prepares the way, goes ahead of us, opens the right doors: "Do not be afraid or discouraged, for the LORD will personally go ahead of you. He will be with you; he will neither fail you nor abandon you" (Deuteronomy 31:8 NLT).

I remember, too, the prayers of the Congolese mothers who sat beside me to comfort me day and night, quietly and wordlessly. They were mothers who knew the pain and sorrow of losing their own babies. We were a sisterhood of sorrowing mothers. But I also have the beautiful memory, too, of returning to the Congo years later, with our baby Ruth in my arms (she is presently a doctor herself) and how these Congolese women proclaimed, "We are all her mothers!"

Ruth E. Berggren, MD

RUTH BERGGREN, MD, MACP, directs the Center for Medical Humanities & Ethics at University of Texas Health, San Antonio. In this role, she teaches ethics and professionalism while nurturing empathy and humanitarian values.

Dr. Berggren arrived at UT Health San Antonio in fall 2006 after an eventful stint at New Orleans' Charity Hospital, where she stood by patients in the HIV ward during Hurricane Katrina until all were safely evacuated. She was named director of the Center for Medical Humanities & Ethics in October 2007.

The daughter of public health physicians, Ruth spent her childhood in Haiti, where she grew up speaking French and Creole and dreamed of becoming a marine biologist. She studied biology and humanities at Oberlin College, later attending Harvard Medical School and completing internal medicine training at Massachusetts General Hospital. Board-certified in internal medicine and infectious diseases, Ruth has extensive experience in clinical AIDS and viral hepatitis care and research, as well as HIV care in resource-poor settings. As an educator, she delights in creating transformational experiential learning opportunities for health professionals through community-service learning, globally and locally. Most recent, she has been a committed responder to the COVID-19 pandemic as a member of San Antonio's Health Transition Team and a special adviser to Bexar County.

Married to her husband, Tyler, for thirty-three years, Ruth is proud to be the mother of Alex and Megan Curiel.

Presence

There's a feeling that I get sometimes, early in the morning just before dawn. You have to get up intentionally early to capture it—a sense that all is well with the world, everything is going to go well, and the coming day is full of potential. No part of the day has been lost or wasted…yet. It's a whole and perfect day that is getting itself ready. There's a quiet inside and out: no noise from the highway or the radio, with birds just barely stirring.

I dug deep this morning to search for the origins of this feeling—when had I first learned to recognize it? I was transported back to my early childhood in rural Haiti, living on the grounds of the Albert Schweitzer Hospital with my physician parents in the Artibonite Valley. We lived there because they believed that all people, regardless of their circumstances, should have a chance to live a full and healthy life. They felt responsible to work toward that vision in a humble valley of a tiny country where the barriers to human flourishing are especially high due to poverty, preventable diseases, and human dysfunction. For years my father focused on getting tetanus vaccine to women in the marketplaces, eventually proving that three jabs to women of reproductive age would eradicate the scourge of neonatal tetanus that for centuries had wasted the lives of countless Haitian newborns.

Dad always got up to be well on his way before the dawn on market days. It was the only way to ensure that the caravan of vaccine- and health worker-laden jeeps would make it over the unpaved, rutted roads before the searing sun melted the ice in the insulated vaccine boxes. Sometimes I would see him with my mother, reading candlelit Scripture and saying a quiet prayer before he left to lead his team. Those were moments of cool and calm—full of potential, unsullied. Many hours later, he'd come home gritty and sweaty, scooping me and my sister up, one in each arm as we joyfully screeched and dodged the brim of his scratchy straw hat.

My parents carved family time away from public-health endeavors on weekends. Up before dawn, we would load the jeep with provisions for the beach near the fishing town of St. Marc. Well known for its coral reefs, plentiful fish, and colorful sea fans, St. Marc was home to one of the largest deep-sea sponges in the Caribbean—perhaps one of the largest in the world. The aquatic environment of Haiti was pristine in those days. Fishermen paddled hand-hewn wooden canoes to cast their nets, and we would spend all morning snorkeling and marveling at nature.

I treasured those one-on-one moments snorkeling with my dad. Holding my hand, he'd swim away from my mother's worried admonitions with his large fins churning bubbles in wakes behind us. We'd escape to a magical world extravagantly adorned with giant cascades of coral, dive deep to peer into the crevasses, seek to glimpse a tiny orange seahorse next to a pink sea anemone or a brooding octopus. Occasionally we'd stop and simply float on our stomachs to watch the parades of tropical fish and observe what might unfold. I'd get that feeling again in those moments—the sense that all is well, all is exactly as it should be: nature unfolding its perfection, and we immersed within it. I remember the sound of our breathing through the snorkel tubes. This was all we could hear. The sound of the breath—reliable and predictable. No other sounds at all other than lapping water from the gentle wavelets rocking our floating bodies.

Occasionally I'd tense up at a threat, frightened by an uninvited jellyfish or a gleaming barracuda. In those moments I'd feel Dad's warm hand firmly grasping mine and gently keeping me still or steering me away from the stinging tentacles. We'd swim to another spot, and I'd occasionally glance up at the sky from under the water. Blinding, shining light refracted off a thousand tiny bubbles in the aqua-clear water. I'd turn my head back downward to see what new discoveries might loom from below, hear our rhythmic breathing through the snorkel tubes, and tighten my grip on Dad's hand.

"You are safe," his warm grip seemed to say in return. "You are safe, we are meant to be here, I am with you, and all shall be well."

Psalm 19 was one of Dad's favorites. He had committed the King James version to memory and enjoyed repeating it for us often whenever we spent time in nature, and especially at the beach in Haiti, or during a spectacular sunrise or sunset.

The heavens declare the glory of God;
the skies proclaim the work of his hands.
Day after day they pour forth speech;
night after night they reveal knowledge.
They have no speech, they use no words;
no sound is heard from them.
Yet their voice goes out into all the earth,
their words to the ends of the world.
In the heavens God has pitched a tent for the sun.
It is like a bridegroom coming out of his chamber,
like a champion rejoicing to run his course.
It rises at one end of the heavens
and makes its circuit to the other;
nothing is deprived of its warmth." (Psalm 19:1–6 NIV)

The Story of Keisha

KEISHA WAS ONE of my patients in New Orleans' Charity Hospital in August 2005. I've changed her name for this story, choosing one with both African and Hebrew origins. Keisha, from *Qetsi'ah,* is a name that references Cassia—a tree with vibrant yellow flowers. The name references Keziah, a daughter of Job, and is also derived from Lakeisha, a "created name from African-American culture, a form of Aiesha or Aisha: Life (ah-EE-sha—Arabic, North Africa; Swahili, East Africa)"; also…"a form of Letitia: Great joy (Latin)."[1]

Keisha had full-blown AIDS, as we infectious disease doctors call it when the human immunodeficiency virus (HIV) has destroyed so many CD4 immune cells (T-cells), that a person is vulnerable to opportunistic infections. Without regular access to health care, full-blown AIDS has a lethal prognosis, with risks of cancer, wasting, blindness, and inevitable death. In 2005 we already had miraculous combinations of pills, called highly active anti-retrovirals, that eventually reverse most of HIV's damage to the immune system. People with HIV should be able to live full lives, pursue careers, and create families. But even in the era of anti-retroviral therapy,

[1] The Black Names Project, www.blacknamesproject.com.

full-blown AIDS is perilous, and medicine cannot reconstitute the immune system overnight. Healing takes time.

Keisha was much too young to have full-blown AIDS. Her exceedingly low T-cell count suggested her immune system had likely been suppressed for a very long time. Still in her early twenties, Keisha was infected when she was far too young to understand what a virus was or capable of protecting herself. She only knew that the word *AIDS* was synonymous with shame.

Keisha did not attend the local clinic where the healing medicine was available at no cost. It was well-known that the HOP (HIV Outpatient Clinic) had a hot and crowded waiting room in downtown New Orleans. At the HOP, all manner of people huddled together in a modest space and worried that they would either be seen by a neighbor or risk having their name be called out loud. Keisha found it unbearable. With her HIV silent and forgettable for many years, she pursued other aspects of her life. She enrolled in a master's degree program that would allow her to become a professional. She lived under the radar with her asymptomatic HIV until one day her kidneys failed and she needed dialysis. Kidney failure and low T-cells compounded Keisha's risk of infection. And so it was that she landed with fever at the Healing Place (Charity Hospital's ninth-floor ward for immunosuppressed people) two days before Hurricane Katrina struck New Orleans.

From the get-go, Keisha's mother never left her side. She slept on a pallet of sofa cushions and blankets next to the hospital bed, sitting up to pay close attention whenever our team made rounds. We were searching for the cause of Keisha's fever and holding out the promise of initiating immune-restoring medicines as soon as the fever source was controlled. After rounds, mom would get out her cell phone and call family with a progress report. From what I could overhear, Keisha had prayers from many unseen supporters.

There had been ample notice that a devastating hurricane was bearing down on steamy New Orleans. For days I heard pounding hammers in our uptown neighborhood as people protected property and boarded-up windows. Fuel-station lines stretched for blocks with cars packed for the exodus. With two children, a husband, two dogs, and a cat, I had my own family to worry about. But in August 2005 I was assigned to oversee Charity's inpatient HIV service. My husband was responsible for the hematology and medical oncology services at Tulane Hospital. In terse phone calls, medical chiefs informed us Code Gray meant we were to report for hospital duty despite the looming storm. For us, as for Keisha and her mother, fleeing Hurricane Katrina was never an option.

The drama and trauma of Charity for the next six days I have recorded elsewhere, but I must bring you to my defining moment—that moment for which I owe a debt of gratitude to Keisha's mom.

Anxiety for our stranded patients mushroomed as flood waters rose, food became scarce, and the power outage dragged on. Most of my patients had AIDS, many dually diagnosed with mental illness or addiction. There was no one available to consult with me for their care. None of my medical residents had shown up for duty. The storm hit on a Sunday, knocking out power, and emergency power in the hospital was gone after twenty-four hours. The electric IV pumps didn't work. Diagnostic tests could not be ordered.

Dialysis requires electricity. Keisha missed her Monday dialysis and then her Wednesday dialysis. I had no technology to guide me, and I dreaded what might come. I feared that without dialysis, she'd die of electrolyte disturbances from her kidney failure.

Keisha's mom invited me to a prayer service being held in Charity's lobby early Wednesday evening, and we trudged down the slippery-wet hospital stairs together. I looked around to see who was in attendance. There were surgical residents in their blue scrubs, several leaning on the wooden oars they had used to paddle from one hospital to the other. There were old professors and young moms, doctors and nurses, patients in wheelchairs, cleaning staff, food workers, and random family members. Together, we represented the cultural, ethnic, racial, and economic diversities and disparities written into New Orleans history over the centuries. And here we were, a motley congregation of unlikely fellow travelers, all with the same mixture of anxiety, disbelief, and desperate hope written on our faces.

Why were the people of Charity praying in that particular moment? Just beyond the hospital doors, snipers had been sighted taking shots at doctors and nurses attempting to load patients into boats. Three days after the storm, incoming help for Charity patients was nowhere and our attempts at evacuation constantly thwarted. Outside the hospital, the water level was up to our necks. Nearby explosions had started fires and intermittently filled the air with acrid smoke. People were pounding on Charity's doors with their belongings piled on rafts floating behind them, their dogs and children on inner tubes, being turned away at gunpoint by hospital security.

Several people in scrubs began to sing, their resonant, harmonious voices reminiscent of what you might hear in the gospel tent at Jazz Fest. Some of these hospital workers actually had been performers in the gospel tent at Jazz Fest that year. They voiced the words to "We Shall Overcome," the anthem of the civil rights movement whose lyrics spoke to our determination in this moment. We all joined in.

Just then, the hospital chaplain opened a giant Bible and solemnly read the ancient words of Isaiah 43:1–3 to a speechless and stunned assembly:

> But now, this is what the LORD says—
>
> he who created you, Jacob,
>
> he who formed you, Israel:
>
> "Do not fear, for I have redeemed you;
>
> I have summoned you by name; you are mine.
>
> When you pass through the waters,
>
> I will be with you;
>
> and when you pass through the rivers,
>
> they will not sweep over you.

When you walk through the fire,
you will not be burned;
the flames will not set you ablaze
For I am the LORD your God,
the Holy One of Israel, your Savior." (NIV)

Keisha's mom and I clung to each other in that moment, tears streaming down our faces. We were not alone in our weeping. These were not tears of self-pity or despair. Rather, we wept with gratitude, and sheer awe at the Holy Presence made manifest to all of us gathered together in that space and in that moment. We shared a profound sense of connectedness to one another, united by a higher purpose, directly and emphatically linked through the writings of Isaiah to all of humanity throughout the millennia. Amen.

Chris Buckingham

JOHN CHRISTOPHER (CHRIS) Buckingham lives in the Texas Hill Country with his amazingly wonderful wife, Janet, a model woman of God. They have two children and four grandchildren.

Chris used his mechanical engineering skills to conduct research and product development at Southwest Research Institute, where he spent his entire career. Many of his projects included the design and fabrication of major testing facilities that were used to conduct fluid mechanics-related testing for the gas pipeline industry and oil and gas production. He also led a team to design and fabricate specialty compressors that are used to produce water on the International Space Station.

When Chris's career track changed to management,

he surrounded himself with outstanding employees that he led using Christ-centered principles of servant leadership. Besides developing the technical program, Chris focused much of his energy on mentoring and career-development programs, including developing and teaching a career-development program that was rolled out to the entire company.

Upon retirement, Chris immediately began volunteering to lend a hand to people needing help by completing house repairs and building wheelchair ramps. He also enjoys being a mentor and adult role model to a young man who needed a male figure in his life. Chris uses his woodworking talents to turn wooden bowls on his lathe, specializing in segmented bowls. Most of his bowls are given to family and friends, but many are donated to fundraising efforts.

Chris's favorite activity, by far, is spoiling his grandkids.

A Cloud of Witnesses

I GREW UP in a suburb of Baltimore, Maryland, and had just graduated with a mechanical engineering degree from Lehigh University in Pennsylvania. It was Saturday, April 12, 1980, and I landed in San Antonio, Texas, after embarking on a 1,700-mile, three-day solo excursion to start my first job after college. As any new graduate, I was excited to start this new chapter in my life and a career in research and development. However, my story begins many years earlier, and God's fingerprints were all over my journey.

At the tender age of fourteen, my life's path changed dramatically when my father passed away unexpectedly. Living with my father was difficult. He was a demanding man. His expectations for my sisters and me were unreasonably high, and he had a hair-trigger, violent temper. Nevertheless, I still took his death extremely hard. I was the youngest of three children and the only son. Because of this, I felt I needed to become the "man of the house," taking on the typical yardwork, house maintenance, and handyman responsibilities. My amazing and loving mom, Helen Florence Brunk Buckingham (Thomas) (Witness #1), never discouraged this, but she did ensure that I stayed focused on school and

Boy Scout activities.

I loved to go camping with my family, but my first camping trip with the Boy Scouts was not the adventure I had hoped. As a sensitive eleven-year-old, I was homesick. The other boys made fun of me, and the adults did not seem willing to provide me any comfort. As a result, I avoided most of the camping trips and made no progress in learning the skills required to achieve rank advancements. Consequently, soon after my dad died I told Mom that I wanted to quit scouting.

Mom wanted very much for me to continue in scouting, and after learning the reason why I wanted to quit, she found a new troop for me to join. One of the leaders of that troop, Tom Rosso (Witness #2), lived down the street, and I sometimes played with his son. Soon after joining the new troop, I hesitantly went on another camping trip. On the first full day, those homesick feelings returned. However, Mr. Rosso recognized my struggle and pulled me aside. We walked together for a while, and I felt better. I do not remember exactly what he said that day, but I never got homesick again. Soon I was thriving in the new troop and on my way to much bigger outings—eventually attaining the rank of Eagle Scout.

Only months after joining my new Scout troop, I got the opportunity to go on a weeklong, high-adventure hiking trip to Philmont Scout Ranch in New Mexico. That was a dream opportunity, and I began raising funds to pay for the trip and acquire the needed equipment. However, I needed transportation to attend the planning meetings in downtown Baltimore and to participate in the many training hikes.

In stepped Calvin O. McElhattan Jr. (Witness #3), or Uncle Mac. An uncle by marriage, he was a rough-around-the-edges, hard-working employee of a tree service company who often worked nights spraying trees in highway medians. Uncle Mac had a generous spirit—demonstrated by his twenty-five-year service as a volunteer ambulance driver for the Reisterstown Volunteer Fire Department—and he was there for me when I needed him. He made sure that I was at every meeting and was my "drop-off" and "pick-up" for every training hike. Uncle Mac surely helped me find my way when the loss of my father was still fresh.

Once my scouting course was on track, Mom decided that my spiritual life needed attention and I needed to become involved in a Christian-based organization. During the 1950s, my dad (with my mom as a volunteer) drove a non-air-conditioned school bus full of high school kids to Young Life's Frontier summer camp in Colorado. In the spring after Dad died, Mom was very excited when she heard that a new Young Life chapter was opening for the students at my high school. John and Pat Gerstmyer (Witnesses #4 and #5) were high school teachers in a neighboring town who felt the call to start the Young Life chapter, and I attended regularly right from the beginning. On a Young Life weekend in New Jersey, on a Friday night, the speaker talked about Jesus and I had questions—questions my friends could not answer. So, I spoke with John.

I didn't get all my questions answered that weekend, but the next week John and Pat started separate Bible studies for the boys and girls enrolled in Young Life. Since I was the only boy in the Bible study, John was able to direct all his energy to help me understand what it meant to give my life to Christ. He walked me through a booklet by Robert Boyd Munger, *My Heart, Christ's Home*. One day that summer, as I was praying while cutting a neighbor's lawn, I accepted Christ into my life. By the time I was a senior, our weekly Young Life meetings included up to one hundred students. The Gerstmyers were very influential in the lives of many high school students, including my sister and me!

During my senior year of high school, my neighbor told me that he had a friend, Mr. Bryant (Witness #6), who was building a marble-dust tennis court (not a common surface). The construction process included a lot of tedious and strenuous work making forms, moving marble dust, spreading, screeding, rolling, and patching, and then doing it repeatedly. I agreed to work with Mr. Bryant, and we spent many Saturdays completing his project.

Although I do not remember much of what we talked about, I do remember one conversation like it was yesterday. When he asked what I was doing after graduation, I told him about my plans to attend a well-respected liberal arts college about twenty minutes from home. I remember telling him that I was going to live at home because my mother needed me and I was not ready to move away.

In his easy tone, he told me how important it was for him to have attended college away from home. Besides allowing him to grow, more important, he met his wife! He encouraged me to step out of my comfort zone when the opportunity arose. Two years later, that conversation was a major influence in my decision to transfer to Lehigh University (3.5 hours away) to pursue a degree in mechanical engineering. Then, almost three years after that, I had the courage to take a dream job in Texas.

Without question, my most influential professor at Lehigh University was Dr. Jerzy Owczarek (Witness #7), a fast-talking man with a thick Polish accent. I first met him during my fluid mechanics course, where I had to quickly adapt my learning style to his teaching style. When I was struggling to understand the class material, I gathered the courage to visit Dr. Owczarek in his office. Although he was busy with his own work, he cleared his worktable, pulled up a second chair, and said, "Let's see what we can figure out." Other professors made me feel like I was bothering them, and they offered little to no help, but Dr. Owczarek showed that he cared about me as a person and a student—and also offered helpful career advice. I was lucky to be able to take a second course from Dr. Owczarek. It is not surprising that, throughout my career, my specialties in mechanical engineering were gleaned from the courses taught by Dr. Owczarek.

So, back to Saturday, April 12, 1980… I began that new dream job in San Antonio. Everything worked out well—a huge understatement since I met an intelligent and beautiful woman (Janet Elaine Peters) on my first day at work and married her almost two years later. The job also worked out fairly well, since I retired from that same company after thirty-eight years of service.

The apostle Paul tells us in Hebrews 12:1, "Therefore, since we are surrounded by such a great cloud of witnesses, let us throw off everything that hinders and the sin that so easily entangles. And let us run with perseverance the race marked out for us" (NIV). Thank you, Mom, Mr. Rosso, Uncle Mac, Mr. Bryant, John and Pat Gerstmyer, and Dr. Owczarek, for your special influences in the direction of my life. I thank God that He sent you as a cloud of witnesses in my life.

Seven witnesses! Hmmm, that seems to be an important number in the Bible. Just a coincidence, I guess.

Jesus In My Heart

THROUGH A CONNECTION with Young Life, I accepted Jesus as my Lord and Savior when I was fourteen years old, and my relationship with God grew through high school, college, and as an adult. However, my faith journey got a large jolt when I attended a Walk to Emmaus weekend. The purpose of this weekend was to experience Christian renewal and equip church members to become Christian leaders in their churches, homes, work, and communities.

Mark tells us to "Love the Lord your God with all your heart and with all your soul and with all your mind and with all your strength" (12:30 NIV). Earlier, I said that I accepted Christ into my life at fourteen, but twenty-five years later I determined that, although I had accepted him with my *mind*, I needed to further accept Christ with all my *heart* and all my *soul* and all my *strength*.

Just after my Walk weekend, I was talking with the associate pastors at my church about finding a way to serve the church and community. Because I had expertise in building decks, making wooden toys, and being an overall handyman, they suggested I use those skills to help people in our small town with house repairs. I thought that this was a good fit for me, and the Housing

Repair Team (HRT) was born, with the mission to offer free gifts from God to our neighbors in need.

My expectation was that we would be helping elderly church members by replacing leaky toilet flappers. This was *my* plan, but God had a more grandiose plan. The first project for the HRT was to complete the construction of a house that had been started but stopped ten years earlier. A mother and her special-needs adult son were living in a dilapidated home adjacent to the new house, whose construction had been started by relatives. The exterior shell, siding, windows, roof, and many of the interior walls were completed. I had never done anything like this, so you can imagine how my prayer life was put into high gear seeking guidance for the successful planning and execution of this project.

Over the next several months, the HRT volunteers worked every weekend to complete this house. In addition to the funding and volunteers provided by our church, companies from the community stepped up to provide electrical work, sheetrock taping and floating, kitchen cabinets, and central air conditioning at no cost. Members of the church donated all of the furniture, bedding, curtains, and kitchen utensils to furnish the house. The mother and son moved into their new home just weeks before Christmas 1996.

About one month after they moved in, as I was preparing for a house blessing, I learned that the towel bar in the bathroom was falling. When the house was decorated, the towel bar was dressed as you might see in a nice hotel—two full-size towels, two hand towels, and two washcloths, beautifully draped over the bar. When I checked on the towel bar to determine the tools I needed, I noticed that the towels looked just like we had laid them. I decided when I went back to re-hang the towel bar that I would let them know they could actually *use* the towels. However, when I returned, I found that the still neatly folded towels were very wet. It turns out that they were so proud of the gift that they had been given that they were keeping it the same as it was received. What a touching tribute to those who were God's hands and feet.

During subsequent projects, I learned the power of having faith that God would provide. We started projects that required skills, volunteers, and funding that were not fully available. I learned to trust that God would see us through the projects, and He always came through. I also learned to be creative when asking for funds. I was singing in the choir the day I was to speak to the congregation about the HRT's need for additional funding. I decided to give my speech in my choir robe. After introducing myself, I asked the crowd if they ever wondered what choir members wore under their robes. I opened my robe to reveal that I was wearing my fully stocked tool belt. Other members of the choir held up hammers, screwdrivers, and cordless tools. The generous congregation donated all the money we needed.

When I reconnected with a high-school friend and she asked me what I was doing, I told her about my work with the HRT and that "this is what God put me on the earth to do." Starting the Housing Repair Team was a defining moment in my life. It brought together my skills in construction, leadership, and project management, all of which I learned along the way at work, at home, and through other volunteer opportunities. Many years later, I am still giving to those in our community.

I am thankful to those who encouraged me to attend the Walk to Emmaus, and those who worked so hard that weekend to show the love of Christ. I am grateful for God moving in me that weekend to encourage me to find a new way to serve His kingdom and for His faithfulness to the HRT ministry. I am also thankful to those who made the Housing Repair Team successful.

Dr. Ricky Burk

A NATIVE OF Lubbock, Texas, Ricky Burk is a graduate of Southwestern University in Tucson, Arizona. He holds the MTh from Liberty Bible College in Pensacola, Florida and DMin from Perkins School of Theology at Southern Methodist University.

Ricky's mission statement for life is to "build the body of Christ by communicating biblical principles." His love for the local church led him to pastor churches in Mississippi and Texas over the course of nearly forty years. His heart to teach and mentor young clergy led him to teach pastoral leadership at Perkins.

Ricky enjoys hiking, fishing, and birding. He and his wife, Beverly, live in the beautiful Texas Hill Country surrounded by God's great outdoors. They relish spending time with their five married children and nine grandchildren and are always looking for ways to continue building the body of Christ.

The Pit of Pity

> "Self-pity is easily the most destructive of the non-pharmaceutical narcotics; it is addictive, gives momentary pleasure and separates the victim from reality." John W. Gardner

> "Give thanks to the LORD, for he is good; his love endures forever." (1 Chronicles 16:34 NIV)

WE STARED AT the neurologist in disbelief. "Would you repeat that last word?" I asked, my head spinning. *Parkinson's.* That was the name we had feared. Now we were facing the battle of our lives.

My wife soon had multiple doctor appointments weekly. As she was unable to drive, I became the mandatory chauffeur for all trips. There was no escaping the wasted time in traffic and waiting rooms. And those rooms were always filled with hurting and unhappy people. Trips to the pharmacy became as routine as getting the mail. Daily monitoring of her medications grew to be a trying responsibility. Her tremors and restless legs kept me awake at night. Her nightmares and sleep walking began to increase. I learned to sleep with one eye and ear open.

My love for my wife is great, and I was trying hard to

be faithful, yet caregiving felt overwhelming. It seemed my life was no longer my own. I felt there was no longer any time for a morning devotional, exercise, lunch with a friend, or a walk in God's great outdoors. I felt I was losing myself. And I felt a victim of unfair circumstances. Why had this happened just as I was nearing retirement? What about plans to travel and spend time with grand-kids? And I wondered why so few seemed to notice my suffering. Or why no one expressed admiration for how I carried my great burden of mistreatment. In the fog of these feelings, I had a defining moment. I was now in another battle. One with self-pity.

It's a battle we've all fought. And we all know the fallout to ourselves and others. How it harms our emotional health and distorts our view of reality. It expects to be served. Feels it is owed. Expects to be praised. Demands it gets its way. Believes it has the right to react negatively to unmet desires. Our own suffering is all we think about in our self-absorbed state. Which is why we rarely see the Enemy coming. It's only once we're under siege that we recognize it.

In order to defeat it, we must begin by genuinely feeling what we feel. If we try to deny our hurt, we only stuff the real emotions deep down inside. And suppression always leads to depression. It stops us from feeling empowered to find solutions and achieving what we want in the long term. It's not good for us or others because the emotions are likely to resurface at an unexpected time. We must allow ourselves to honestly feel what we are feeling.

Yet if we stay in the pit of pity too long, it becomes a difficult one to climb out of. We must move on to replace those self-pitying thoughts with something else. And that something is gratitude. The Oxford Dictionary defines the word grateful as "showing an appreciation of kindness." It is an action to make a choice, and gratitude is the choice. It is a choice to be aware of the gifts and goodness of God all around us. Of the people who love us and help us. It is being grateful for what we have instead of striving for more.

Melodie Beattie said it well: "Gratitude unlocks the fullness of life. It turns what we have into enough, and more. It turns denial into acceptance, chaos into order, confusion into clarity. It can turn a meal into a feast, a house into a home, a stranger into a friend. Gratitude makes sense of our past, brings peace for today, and creates a vision for tomorrow."

These are choices we can all make. They are choices that promote hope and optimism. Healing and peace. Joy and encouragement. They manifest love, devotion, and commitment toward those who mean the most to us. These are choices that can create for all of us powerful and positive defining moments.

Gratitude is the appropriate response to the saving and keeping grace of God. Paul reminds us, "Give thanks in all circumstances; for this is God's will for you in Christ Jesus" (1 Thessalonians 5:18 NIV). Gratitude is a choice of thankfulness for all we have—our life, freedom, nature, friends and family, and so much more. All we have is a gift of God.

The Bible reminds us to give thanks *in* every circumstance, not *for*, because God can bring good out of bad things. Promises out of pain. Blessings out of suffering. God can turn crucifixions into resurrections. This is why we can choose to always be grateful in every circumstance.

A dear friend of mine is the personification of this great truth. His life has been a towering example of maintaining an attitude of gratitude in all circumstances. He has known divorce, battled cancer, experienced a stroke and the loss of an internal organ. Yet he is always to be found with a heart of gratitude. Always giving thanks *in* all circumstances. His grateful spirit rubs off on me and everyone around him. His productivity of Christian ministry is inspirational. His circumstances have given him opportunity for many choices. He has always chosen gratitude. And because of him I am reminded to do the same, that God may be at work in me to make me more like Christ.

It is with a heart of overwhelming gratitude that I can share that my wife is doing better. Gifted medical professionals and physical therapists, the prayers of family and friends, and God's wonderful gift of medicine have all worked together to strengthen her mind and body. Now we enjoy evenings out for dinner. Trips to see our children and grandchildren. Time with friends over food and fellowship. With hearts of gratitude, we are thanking God for even more improvement to come.

So, I have chosen to no longer ask, "God, why is this happing to me?" Instead, I'm choosing to ask, "God, what do you want me to learn from this?" For when we choose to learn from God, we have chosen to become more like Jesus Christ. And gratefulness opens the door to this wonderful opportunity.

Ricky the Rhino

"Life is 10% what happens to you and 90% how you react to it." Charles Swindoll

"Even if my father and mother abandon me, the LORD will hold me close." (Psalm 27:10 NLT)

ANYONE WHO HAS lived through elementary-school recess knows the anxiety of waiting to be picked for the kickball game. The fear of being rejected and the pain it brings can be experienced far too early in life. My introduction came on the school playground as a fourth-grader trying out for the flag football team.

I was filled with anxiety as we gathered around legendary Coach Eubanks. Would I make the team? I knew all my friends were sure to be selected. Would I be left out? As I looked at the other boys, I suddenly realized I was the pudgiest. Everyone else looked lean and firm. I looked down and sucked in my belly. It was then I realized my blue jeans looked different than the others. I was so rotund that my mom had to buy a waist size meant for older boys with longer legs. That meant I had to roll up my pant legs several times. No one else wore their blue jeans the way I did. And I didn't want to stand out. I wanted to fit in.

The tryout was brief, and with great relief we learned everyone would make the team. Next, we heard our coach announce that the moment had come. It was time for the christening. The sacred moment. As third-graders we had stood at a distance to watch this hallowed event. We had listened with awe as the older boys described their life-changing moment. Now it was our turn.

Coach would call each boy's name, and we would take a three-point stance one yard from a blocking dummy he held. The goal was to knock it into the street and hear Coach say no one had ever hit it so hard. We would attack the bag at the sound of his whistle. And at that moment, he would christen each of us with a nickname. It was a title we would carry throughout our school years.

My best friend Jeff went first. We held our breath and then gasped as we heard "Jeff the Giant!" Next my friend Steve took his stance. The whistle blew, and we heard "Steve the Stallion!" Coach was being unusually gracious this year, and now I was next. I dug in both feet and waited for the whistle. At the sound I leapt at the blocking dummy with all my might, and in midair, I heard "Ricky the Rhino."

The air exploded with laughter. All my friends fell on the ground laughing hysterically. I felt the red creep over my face, and I looked away in shame. The pain of the moment seared my brain. I wanted to run away and never be heard of again. Coach Eubanks meant well, as the name was meant to describe someone strong. Me and my friends could only picture a fat beast.

Rejection had hit me head on, much harder than I had hit that blocking dummy, scarring my psyche. My self-image became skewed. For years there was a part of me that continued to think I was fat. An inner voice kept telling me to lose weight. I could not erase the mental image of the pudgy nine-year-old kid fighting back tears while his friends held their sides from laughing so hard.

Rejection is painful. The brain responds to social pain in a similar way it responds to physical pain. Brain pathways activated by physical pain are also activated by social pain. Receptor systems in the brain release natural painkillers when an individual experiences rejection, the same when physical pain occurs. The mental pain of rejection is as real as physical pain.

And it's a pain we've all felt. A criticizing social media post. Not being invited to a party no matter our age. Being turned down for a desired position. A rejection letter from a college. Your ideas and suggestions being ignored at a business meeting. A Dear John letter. As far as your brain is concerned, a broken heart is not so different from a broken arm.

Where can we find healing for this brokenness? An ER for an arm, but what for the heart? The journey for me began by acknowledging the pain. We may not want to admit someone has been able to hurt us, but denying or minimizing the pain will only prolong it. It's always best to deal with uncomfortable emotions by facing them head-on.

Then show yourself a little compassion. Instead of saying to yourself, "You were so stupid to think/believe/suggest/try...," use your inner voice to send a kinder, more affirming message. Speak to yourself like a trusted friend. Forgive yourself for mistakes and failures. It's never helpful to keep punishing ourselves for regrets we may have.

Then take a step back and reflect. What can you learn? Did the person intend to hurt you, or was it your reaction that caused the pain? How can you grow so a similar response is not repeated? If it was intended, ask yourself if it really matters. Was the rejection from a person you don't necessarily care about or from someone who matters to you?

Above all remember the fundamental reason rejection hurts: it makes us feel we are unlovable. We all have an insatiable need to be loved. It's a basic human need and necessary to be a healthy individual. Yet love from others is inconsistent. No person or group of persons can love us as fully and completely as we need to be loved. If we expect it, we are headed for disappointment.

The unfailing love we need comes from God: "Give thanks to the God of heaven. His faithful love endures forever" (Psalm 136:26 NLT). We can always depend on God to love us. Human love, at its best, is circumstantial. God's love is faithful and constant, loving us in every circumstance. It never fails us.

Ricky the Rhino is now a distant memory. That scared, shamed, pudgy little boy has been healed by embracing God's great love. His self-image is now based on how God sees him, not how others view him. His need for human love has more realistic expectations. And he is no longer dependent on others to accept or reject him. He has been healed.

People may reject you, but God will never reject you. God will always love you unconditionally. So, embrace it. For the healing of rejection that you need.

Rachael M. Colby

Born and raised in Jamaica, award-winning writer Rachael M. Colby resides in Cape Cod, Massachusetts. Wife, mom, beach bum, artist, work in progress, avid tweeter—#HealthyFaithChat leader. Rachael writes to glorify God, encourage believers, and reach the lost. She connects culture's questions with Christianity's answers, inspires faith, and motivates through articles, devotions, poetry, and interviews. She has a heart for reconciliation and to uplift those who serve in tough places.

Her work has appeared on *Southern Ohio Christian Voice*, Inkspirations Online, and the Blue Ridge Mountains Christian Writers Conference Blog; in the compilation books *Creative Writing Journal: Faith-Inspired Writing Prompts & Hope-Filled Poetry* and *The Courage to*

Write: 62 Devotions to Encourage Your Writing Journey; and in the *Oak Ridger* newspaper. Rachael's works in progress include a compilation of her family's and others' stories of their work as civil-rights activists and life during the integration of Oak Ridge, Tennessee, in the 1960s, a devotional for writers, and a children's picture book.

Rachael's awards include the North Carolina Christian Writers Conference Tar Heel Award for articles and poetry, the Ohio Christian Writers Conference Blue Seal Award for articles and devotions, the Blue Ridge Mountain Christian Writers Conference Foundation Award in the articles, poetry, and devotions categories, and she was a 2022 Selah Award winner for her article in print "The Integration of Oak Ridge."

Rachael runs on copious amounts of coffee and chocolate and a whole lot of "Help me, Jesus."

Website: TattooItOnYourHeart.com
Twitter: @RachaelColby7
Facebook: Rachael M Colby
Instagram: rachaelmcolby

Three Men, Jesus, and Me

IT WASN'T THE first time suicide knocked on my door. I vowed growing up that I wouldn't fall into the same pit as some of my loved ones. I didn't want to repeat their mistakes. Why, at twenty years old, did my life lay in shambles?

Sometimes as a little girl in the night's hush, I'd look up in wonder at the star-studded skies and I'd ask Jesus questions, but I didn't know Him.

Growing up with my grandparents in Jamaica, Billy Graham was the salute to my Sunday mornings. I'd race into their room and curl up at the foot of the bed, and Grandpa would reach for the old wooden radio atop his dresser. With a twist and a click of the knob, it burst to life with "This is Billy Graham coming to you live…" and George Beverly Shea singing, "How Great Thou Art." And we'd listen to Billy preach before we went to the little stone church with the stained-glass window of the Good Shepherd bringing home the one lost sheep.

That sheep is me, I thought.

After church, Grandpa and I sat in his sun-dappled chair on the verandah and sang "Once in Royal David's City" and "All Things Bright and Beautiful" out of his old worn hymnal. Treasured times.

Then, many upheavals. Canada with my mom, back to Jamaica, my stepmother left my dad and took my little brothers with her, boarding school, and back with my dad. Turbulent teen years.

School provided a good academic education and a disciplined environment, but I argued much of their doctrine. They couldn't answer my questions. Well intentioned in my quest for truth but lost in my sin, had I died then, I wouldn't have made heaven.

The rifts in my family weighed on me. I felt I wasn't allowed to love them all, like I had to choose. I feared rejection. I battled suicide. Perhaps, I hoped, when I launched out on my own, took control of my circumstances, life would become stable.

I burned my journal with my letters to God when I eloped at eighteen and moved to Pensacola, Florida. I possessed everything I wanted, or it was within reach, yet I woke at night feeling hollow, like the wind could blow through me.

Two years later, life felt like a landslide: My husband left, the marriage ended. Estranged from my mother, I bore the pain of separation from my siblings. Hope faltered. I heard the words recorded in the Bible that Job's wife had spoken to him: "Curse God and die!" (2:9 NLT).

I fell to my knees, weeping. "No," I said. "God, I will not curse You. I still believe in You. Help me."

How did this magazine land here? I mused when I checked my mailbox later. It was near impossible for the mail carrier to mistake the apartment buildings. The Billy

Graham Evangelistic Association's *Decision* magazine catapulted me to childhood memories of Billy preaching the gospel and how it captivated and comforted me.

The address label indicated the magazine subscriber lived on the opposite side of the complex. "Hello," I called him and said, "I have your Billy Graham magazine. But I'd like to read it for a minute before I give it to you, if you don't mind." He chuckled, and we arranged a time to meet by the pool, which separated our buildings, but I never showed up. I was so caught up reading, his knock startled me. I opened the door to meet the gentle smile of Rev. George Horton, a retired Baptist minister, my first face-to-face witness.

Rev. Horton and his sweet wife, Evelynn, took me under their wing and to church at Pensacola Christian College. They opened their home to me often. I knew they loved me; their presence convicted me. I respected and feared hurting them, which kept me from some bad decisions and out of much trouble. They answered my myriad of questions, but I didn't quite grasp salvation.

I chucked the Bible the Hortons gave me on the dresser. There was no room in my suitcase. I intended to run from life, pretend I was fine, party, and pursue my modeling career while working at my host's ice cream parlor in Cape Cod, Massachusetts, during the summer of 1987. But to my dismay, I discovered on arrival that my hosts were a bunch of Jesus fanatics. Trapped. As their guest, I reluctantly accompanied them to church. They shared the gospel, and I called them every name in the book at the top of my lungs.

"I'm a good person. I'm good enough for God." I said, "I've been through enough hell here on earth, God has to let me into heaven!"

"For all have sinned and fall short of the glory of God," they shared from the Bible (Romans 3:23 NIV). We're saved by grace through faith. Salvation is the gift of God, not works, they explained (see Ephesians 2:8–9).

Appalled and confused why I'd turned so mean, I dreamt of and awoke to the echo of the lyrics from the church rock band's song based on John 3:3, which says: "Jesus replied, 'I tell you the truth, unless you are born again, you cannot see the Kingdom of God'" (NLT). But I didn't let on.

I feared if I called my sin "sin," all I'd have left was regret. But how does one argue with Jesus and win?

"Unless you repent you will all likewise perish" (Luke 13:3 NKJV).

I searched the Scriptures. Jesus leaves no gray areas. We either embrace all of Him or reject Him.

I threatened to leave, but the familiar message drew me.

Except for me and a kid named Dana, everyone who worked at the ice-cream parlor was a Jesus fanatic or a tie-dyed follower of the Grateful Dead band. I wasn't sure which was crazier. I replaced the tract in the display by the window where the line of customers stood.

"You'll be one of them by summer's end," Dana said.

"I will never get saved!"

I had no intention of "getting saved" when I knelt at the altar a week later in response to a sermon about the man who asked Jesus to help his unbelief (see Mark 9:23–24). But what had I to lose? So, I repented of my sin, asked Jesus into my heart, and became born again. "Wait!" I said when my new friend who prayed with me rose. "I came up to pray for faith."

After weeks of silence, I called Rev. Horton. "Hello," I said, "I got baptized today."

He chuckled and said, "Tell me about it."

These three men added many defining moments to my life.

Grandpa laid a foundation, so years later I recognized truth when I encountered the gospel again.

Rev. Billy Graham was a stepping-stone on my road to salvation, someone sure in a shaky world. He stood on the Rock—the foundation of all eternity, Jesus—and stayed faithful to preach His Word, the message of our need for repentance, God's love for us, and His offer of grace and salvation: new life.

The Hortons and I stayed in touch. Through the years, though miles apart and months between calls, Rev. Horton always answered the phone as if he expected my call. "Hello!" I'd say. He'd chuckle and without a pause continue to minister to me as if he had a front-row view of my life.

Suicide is a permanent mistake for a temporary problem. Waking up in hell is worse than anything you're going through. Without Christ, life's burdens are too heavy. Even when I filled up on all the good life offered, it left me lacking.

Jesus is the answer for all that ails us. He made us for

heaven and a personal relationship with Himself. He never leaves or forsakes and wants to do life with us.

Now I walk the pilgrim path in this house of dust indwelt by God's Spirit. Saved by His grace, led by truth, held in hope and peace, filled with joy not contingent on circumstance, loved by the Savior.

And sometimes in the night's hush, I look up in wonder at the star-studded skies and I ask Jesus questions. I know Him. And I'm grateful.

That Day

ANOTHER BLUE-SKY JAMAICA morning winked through the slatted windows. A canary's song floated from the canopy of our almond tree.

"You awake?" my stepmother, Betty called. "Go to the end of the road and see if your father is gone."

I returned to find Betty throwing clothes into a suitcase. "I'm sorry to leave you here," she said, "but I must go."

Within minutes, Betty was in the car with my brothers. Dark curls sprang off two-year-old Paul's head. Five-year-old Simon, a blur of honey-colored skin and blond hair, jumped on the back seat. I motioned for a kiss. He cracked the window—a peck, an impish grin, and he quickly rolled it up. The car pulled away, the earth bent beneath my bare feet, and my anguished heart split wide open. Gone.

I knew Betty had to leave. I feared someone would end up in jail or dead if she stayed. But these were my father's children too. He loved his sons and had never physically hurt them. Only eleven years old and torn in my loyalties, I gave my stepmother a head start and called my father. He rushed onto the airstrip, but the plane had just taken off with his wife and sons bound for the United States.

A divorce and a restraining order prohibiting my father's communication with his sons ensued. He wrote checks; he sent gifts. I saw them. I couldn't talk to Daddy about Simon and Paul because he became angry and sank into depression for days at the mention of their names. I grieved the loss of my little brothers alone.

Years passed. One day, I glimpsed a slip of paper with Betty's phone number. I jotted it down, tucked it away, and waited. I waited to call until I was eighteen years old and moved to America. It took a year to convince Betty I wasn't working with my father to find her. She said she was afraid. I just wanted to see my brothers.

Betty relented. It was clear she had devoted her life to my brothers. She adored them, and they her, and I was grateful.

We began again, my brothers and me.

Simon and Paul had grown up with painful memories and stories of their father. They resisted a relationship with him and expressed fear of betraying their mother if they pursued one. I never initiated conversations about Daddy but answered my brothers' questions and told them he loved them and had changed. Under my vow to Betty, I didn't tell my father I had contact with his sons until they became adults and permitted me. I enjoyed my relationship with my brothers, but it wasn't enough.

Decades lost, buried anger and bitterness—I worried how harboring such emotions would affect my brothers.

I wept for my father's consequent pain. "God, have

mercy. Grant my father favor."

I longed for reconciliation, but time after time, our hopes were crushed.

Early one Father's Day morning, while Paul prepared to return home from visiting us, I prayed, "Lord, I wish my dad would call right now."

I jumped when the phone rang. "It's your father," I said. "Will you speak to him?"

Paul took the phone, and father and son began again. I was happy, and I praised God. But it wasn't enough.

Several years later, my brothers called to say they were coming to visit with their families. Then Daddy told me he was combining his business trip and vacation during the same timeframe. Not wanting to manipulate, I told them they'd be in town simultaneously, and Daddy would stay with us.

Simon made it clear he wasn't ready to see our father. I understood—it was Simon's decision to make. Still, I prayed for a miracle. Daddy held fast to that hope too.

The time came for my family to leave for dinner at my brothers' vacation condo, but Simon's decision hadn't changed. I wept when I told our father that even though his son and family were only twenty minutes away, he could not see them. It was one of the hardest things I've ever done.

Despite his grief, Daddy rushed to comfort me. "Please don't cry! I have a relationship with Paul," he said. "Maybe I need to be grateful for that and accept Simon's decision. Maybe that will have to be good enough—at least for now." Yet everything in me screamed, *It's not good enough for me!* I drove away in tears.

"God, *why* let us get this close only to dash our hopes again? Lord, *You* said hope deferred makes the heart sick. I am *sick* of being the mediator! Why can't I get over this and go on? I don't know whether this *faith* you gave me is a blessing or a curse! If you're not going to do something, then take my faith away, because it hurts too much."

I shut the door, dried my tears, and put on my smile.

The sun fell in the evening sky, and I retreated to my familiar ritual. Warm soapy water and the clink of clean dishes soothed the raw edges of my soul. Snippets of conversation, the children's laughter drifted from the next room. Then footsteps, and Simon's hand rested on my shoulder. "I want our family to all be together tomorrow," he said.

"Son."

"Dad."

And they embraced for the first time in thirty-six years.

So, Simon and Daddy began again. We were together, our father with all his children and grandchildren, for two glorious sun-filled June days.

"Why'd you change your mind, Simon?" I asked later.

"Because I love you. And I love you because you loved me. You pursued me and never gave up. Besides, we all need forgiveness. God knows I do."

Sometimes reconciliation is messy and complicated.

We made mistakes. But Jesus is faithful, and I found the Bible's instructions and promises hold true: "Above all things have fervent love for one another, for 'love will cover a multitude of sins'" (1 Peter 4:8 NKJV). By God's grace and a miracle, our family began again, and it was enough.

Daddy died unexpectedly the following January.

Jackie K. Cooper

JACKIE K. COOPER has been many things during his life. He has been a singer, lawyer, game-show contestant, actor, TV host, writer, and social-media personality. He sang with a trio in high school, got his law degree from the University of South Carolina, had a one-week run on *The Joker's Wild,* appeared as the assistant mayor of Montgomery in the TV movie *King,* hosted *The Jackie K. Cooper Show* in middle Georgia, has written seven memoirs, and currently is active on YouTube, Instagram, Facebook, Twitter and TikTok.

In 2002 he retired from work as a personnel manager with the United States Air Force and planned to concentrate on his writing. But God had other plans. He had maintained a presence on YouTube where he posted his book and movie reviews. He had an amazing 136 subscribers and felt very successful with that number. Then, an influencer with eight million or more followers gave him a shoutout and he went from 136 to 150,000 subscribers virtually overnight.

This rise in exposure has led to many more speaking opportunities where he presents his message of "Age is only a number." He has found many young people are very receptive to this message and have changed their views of what "old" means.

Jackie's books are *Journey of a Gentle Southern Man, Chances and Choices, Halfway Home, The Bookbinder, The Sunrise Remembers, Back to the Garden*, and *Memory's Mist.* His next memoir, *The Wisdom of Winter,* is due out in 2023.

Jackie can be found online at:

Website: jackiekcooper.com
YouTube: youtube.com/user/JackieKCooper
TikTok: tiktok.com/@jackiekcooper77
Facebook: facebook.com/jackiekcooper7
Twitter: @jackiekcooper
Instagram: jackiekcooper77

Jesus, Take a Seat

WHEN I WAS fourteen my mother died. She died of cancer of the lymph nodes. It was a horrible death and one that stays with me till this day. She was diagnosed in the mid-1950s when a diagnosis of cancer was a death sentence. I don't think I recall anyone who was diagnosed with cancer around this time surviving the disease. So, at an early age I was made aware of cancer and how awful that sickness can be.

My mother's death defined my life for many, many years thereafter. In high school I felt I was known as the boy whose mother had died. I felt sympathy from so many—well-intentioned sympathy. It was a kindness only a small town can show. But more than sympathy I wanted normalcy, and that is something I could not find.

Eventually I did find normalcy in my life as I graduated from law school, served in the military, and got married. At that point I had found just about everything I had been searching for over the span of my lifetime. My wife and I were wonderfully happy, and this wonderment increased with the birth of our two sons.

But life has its ups and downs, and one of our downest downs was when my wife, Terry, had a lymph node on her neck begin to swell. The moment I saw this swollen node I went into panic mode. This was the way my mother's illness had started. This meant we had to have a doctor see her as quickly as possible.

We saw our regular doctor, who referred us to a specialist. The specialist was named Don Rhame. I thought it funny since I had known a young man by that name who had graduated high school with my brother in my hometown of Clinton.

When we went for our first appointment, I was more than surprised to find Dr. Rhame was actually that person I had known in Clinton.

Don knew me, my family, and the particulars of my mother's death. I think that made it easier for me to voice my concerns to him about my fears for Terry's health. He was amazingly comforting and assured me he did not think that the lymph node was cancerous. But he did say we should have it removed. Hearing that brought back another flood of memories, none of them good.

The surgery was scheduled for the next week, and then there were the days following when we waited to hear whether the node was malignant or not. During this time, I prayed and prayed and prayed. My work office was in Macon, thirty miles or more from my home, so I had a fairly long drive each way. I used these drives to speak my prayers and concerns audibly.

I don't know when it was that Jesus became visibly apparent to me, but almost as quickly as I began to audibly pray in the car He was there. This was not a case of "Jesus, take the wheel." This was more "Jesus, take a seat." And He did. He was there, beside me in that car. It is hard to describe what happened. He was there, and I could see him, but I saw a presence rather than a clearly defined vision. Still, I clearly heard his voice, and He was repeating over and over that He was with me.

I am not a man who has visions, and I do not know what exactly this was. Yet, I know it was the most wonderful encounter I have ever had in my life. It calmed me during a time when I thought I couldn't be calmed. And when I shared my experience with my wife, it calmed her also.

The report came back, and the lymph node was negative for cancer. Everything was fine. Life could go back to normal. At least in some ways. Still for me, my life had been changed. I had been a believer before the lymph-node experience. Afterward, I was a confident Christian.

You know how in the Bible you read about those times Jesus appeared to His followers after His death. Or the times in the Old Testament when God would appear in some form to people. Well, I was now one of those to whom Jesus had appeared. I had seen Him. I had felt His presence. I had been comforted by Him.

It is not trivializing this occurrence when every time I hear Carrie Underwood sing "Jesus, Take the Wheel," I think of "Jesus, take a seat." That is exactly what He did. On those drives to Macon and back, He was there with me. Was it a miracle or an actuality? I prefer to think it was an actual miracle.

Not My Voice, But His

WHEN I WAS a little boy, I had a very good singing voice. I was a boy soprano. At least that is what my school choir director called it. I sang at school events and other occasions. Finally, in fifth grade, I was selected to go to the state vocal competition. I was scheduled to sing a song titled "If With All Your Heart." I wasn't worried about competing as I had practiced and practiced the song and was very comfortable with it, even that very high note I had to hit toward the end of the song.

The day arrived and I went on stage to sing for the judges. I jumped right into the song and was doing great until that high note came. My voice cracked as the first indication my voice was changing occurred. It sounded like fingernails scraping on a chalk board. It was bad.

In their write up the judges said I was "a fine young man with a great voice," but their score of B indicated they were aware my boy soprano days were over. Now I was on the road to being a tenor, and that turned out just fine. I sang all the way through high school and college.

After I married, I joined the church choir and had a great time singing there. I would also perform from time to time with my brother, whose voice was very similar to mine. Plus he could harmonize. I couldn't. My brother's problem was he couldn't memorize lyrics. He had to have them on paper in front of him or written on his hand. He just couldn't recall them when we were about to perform. We sang "Tomorrow" from *Annie* one time, and in rehearsal we would sing the very first line about the sun coming out, and then he would ask, "What's next?"

I would say "Tomorrow"—the song's title.

We ended up performing with the lyrics lying on the floor in front of us.

As I got older my voice faded and my singing performances were fewer and fewer. But not everyone knew this. Stephanie didn't. She was the daughter of two of our best friends, and she lived in Charleston, South Carolina. She called one April night to tell me she was engaged and was to be married in Charleston in the fall. It was a semi-long engagement.

Stephanie said she had always dreamed of me singing at her wedding. I responded that though that was very sweet, my singing days were behind me. She did not like that answer and used all the persuasive powers that she put into her law practice to convince me to sing. I finally gave in and said yes. I figured by the fall they might have broken up, or I could possibly come up with a reason not to sing.

After some discussion we agreed I would sing "The Lord's Prayer." Not the easiest of songs and another one with a high note at the end. But at least I was familiar with it. So, I had a friend of mine tape the piano accompaniment, and I started rehearsing as I drove to work each day. I must admit when I was singing in that car, I sounded good. My wife agreed when she was with me on a drive and I sang it for her. I had no fears about the voice being back.

That confidence lasted until we got to Charleston for the wedding rehearsal. Stephanie was getting married in one of the oldest churches in the city. When I asked about a microphone, the minister of music said microphones were not needed since the church was acoustically perfect. His words, not mine. He told me just to come down to the front of the altar and sing my song.

With full confidence I strode down to my appointed spot and began to sing. Even in the beginning part I knew the notes were bad. I could hear dogs howling in the street. As I looked at the audience, I saw my wife had her head bowed. If she was praying, she was praying for it to be over. The groom's family appeared to be in shock. It was a fiasco.

The minister of music suggested we try it in another key. That did not help. I left the church in disgrace with my wife telling me I was going to ruin Stephanie's wedding.

What was I to do? I didn't want to embarrass Stephanie and ruin her wedding, but I also didn't want to back out at the last minute. I resorted to prayer. I prayed to God like I hadn't done in ages. I even offered bargains—I'd be a better person, husband, father, etc. I was still praying when we reached the church the next day.

I did notice no one wanted to look me in the eye. There was a lot of coughing and turning of heads. I think if my wife could have found an excuse to stay at the hotel, she would have. Time, however, marched on, and suddenly it was my time to take my spot. I prayed one last prayer, opened my mouth—and God sang.

He truly did. There was not one missed note. And when I approached that high note, I hit it like a mountaineer scaling the Alps. Onward and upward I went with strength building in every second that passed. The whole thing was operatic and epic.

Afterward, I could hardly believe it, but the entire ceremony was taped, and there was proof of my vocal rendition. People who heard it couldn't believe it. I couldn't believe it. But truth be told I knew deep in my heart and soul that on Stephanie's special day Jackie Cooper opened his mouth and God's voice emerged.

And He is a great singer.

Letha Cole Crouch

LETHA COLE CROUCH has spent the majority of her life creating and worshiping through sacred music.

She grew up as an air force "brat" during and following World War II and lived in ten of the United States, as well as Japan and Germany. Her mother played piano and was a voice major; she had a profound influence on Letha's life.

Letha earned a BA in Piano Performance and studied organ at Southwestern Baptist Theological Seminary. For several summers she played piano at both Glorieta (New Mexico) and Ridgecrest (North Carolina) Baptist Assemblies. She served three years as assistant music editor at the Baptist Sunday School Board in Nashville, TN. During that time, she began composing and publishing sacred music—vocal solos, piano arrangements of hymns, children's cantatas, and choral pieces.

In 1970 she moved to San Antonio, Texas, to become organist and music assistant at the Alamo City's historic First Baptist Church. Also during those years, she taught music at San Antonio Christian School. Her life was greatly enriched by many years as a discussion leader in Bible study fellowship. In retirement, after she was widowed, she moved to live close to and spend time with her daughter's family of four. She enjoys teaching piano to their two teenage sons.

I Am His, and He Is Mine

ALMIGHTY GOD IS personal. Amazingly, wonderfully so. He created each of us uniquely. He numbers the hairs on our heads. He knows our thoughts before we think them. The sinless Lamb of God bore our sins—every sin of every human—on the cross. He *became* my sin, your sin (see 2 Corinthians 5:21)! He is personal. Who can comprehend such an amazing God?

Throughout my life I have been blessed with some very strong One-on-one experiences with my Lord.

Many years ago in a ladies' Bible study, I heard the question, "If you should die tonight, do you know *for certain* that you will go home to heaven?" It was a startling thought. *Yes, I think so! I've gone to church all my life. I read the Bible. I pray. I was baptized many years ago. I even play the organ at church.*

But the words *for certain* continued to bother me. I wanted to know His assurance, His absolute certainty, without a single doubt! So, I got down on my knees, confessed my sin, and asked Him to save me, to make me eternally His. To make me know *for certain* that I belonged to Him.

I did that for several days in a row, confessing, asking His forgiveness and His saving grace. I longed to know for certain that I am eternally His. One day as I said "Amen" and got up off my knees, I sensed that I didn't have to do it anymore. I had peace. He filled my heart and mind with His assurance, confidence, certainty. His peace that passes all understanding. He is mine, and I am His. Eternally.

That experience happened many years ago. Because I am a human, I continue to sin; I need to confess daily, regularly. And He has continued to give me His calming assurance again and again. He comforts my heart with the knowing-without-a-doubt that I am eternally His.

"If we confess our sins, He is faithful and just to forgive us our sins and to cleanse us from all unrighteousness" (1 John 1:9 NKJV).

One particular morning as I was on my knees, bowed down and confessing to Him, I held out my hands, open to him. In them I was yielding my confessed sin. With my eyes closed, I recall the clear mental image of a very large tear-shaped drop of blood coming down from heaven. It descended slowly, slowly, slowly until it landed gently on my hands, completely covering my confessed sin.

Our Savior has paid the price to wash us clean! "But if we walk in the light, as he is in the light, we have fellowship with one another, and the blood of Jesus, his Son, purifies us from all sin" (1 John 1:7 NIV).

The blood of the Passover Lamb is visible to Him over and on the sides of my door! I belong to Him; I am saved. "The blood will be a sign for you on the houses where you are, and when I see the blood, I will pass over you.

No destructive plague will touch you" (Exodus 12:13 NIV).

Another time, driving alone in the car, I was bothered, troubled by something. I was in need of clarity, of guidance. Out loud, in my frustration, I said, "Who can I call to discuss this?" Then in my head I heard His gentle, calm voice saying His personal words to me: "Call to me and I will answer you and tell you great and unsearchable things you do not know" (Jeremiah 33:3 NIV).

He is our personal God, and He is ever ready to listen, to cleanse, to guide. Prayer is always the right answer. Always. "Then you will call on me and come and pray to me, and I will listen to you" (Jeremiah 29:12 NIV).

My prayer for you, dear one, is that you do not simply practice a religion but that you have a personal, loving relationship with the one true God. There is nothing better in this life.

"My sheep listen to my voice; I know them, and they follow me. I give them eternal life, and they shall never perish; no one will snatch them out of my hand" (John 10:27–28 NIV).

God's Song

"I KNOW THE plans I have for you," declares the LORD, "plans to prosper you and not to harm you, plans to give you hope and a future. Then you will call upon me and come and pray to me, and I will listen to you. You will seek me and find me when you seek me with all your heart" (Jeremiah 29:11–13 NIV).

My physical path with God began in California in May of 1943, when I was born to a young air force pilot and his wife.

In God's amazing providence, a future, far distant, part of my life's path also began in November of that same year in Texas, when a godly young man, his wife, and their four children joined First Baptist Church of San Antonio.

People's lives are like songs. God is the composer. He allows us the freedom to modulate, to write our unique stanzas, to improvise in all kinds of ways. But the most beautiful rendition of our lives' songs is always in His key, with His text. Oh, that we would learn to live and sing *His* song!

My mother was a voice major, and she also played piano. She realized early in my life that God had given me an ear for music. She saw to it that I had piano lessons whenever it was possible, so I could read the "language" of music, as well as play it by ear. Sometimes there were holes in the learning during my father's military career. Our family lived in ten different states and two foreign countries prior to my graduation from high school, and I wasn't always able to have piano lessons. But music was my love, so I majored in piano in college. A few years later, through a series of amazing "only God could have done this" events, I was hired to serve as assistant music editor at the Baptist Sunday School Board in Nashville, Tennessee.

In that place I was surrounded by many godly men and women who encouraged and challenged me in wonderful ways. I began to write music: children's songs, anthems, vocal and piano solos. I was blessed to travel to accompany singing at conferences. I played organ at church. It was a rich season in my young life.

God was leading, all the way.

In 1969 the pastor of FBC San Antonio contacted me, asking me to become organist and music assistant for that blessed old church in the heart of the city. I had just prayed about another offer and was certain God was telling me to stay right where I was, in Nashville. Occasionally throughout the next year, however, I heard from the pastor, Dr. Jimmy Allen. Finally, I sensed that I should at least visit the church, to see if God was leading me there. In 1970 He did just that. I was twenty-seven years old.

Becoming a part of the staff at FBCSA was thrilling. The church family was large and healthy, involved in serving our city in all kinds of wonderful ways. We had a huge, dear group of people who served as the sanctuary choir. Playing the organ, undergirding their glorious praise to God week after week, was a joy.

The godly young man and his dear wife who had joined in 1943 (now considerably older) became acquaintances, kind friends. Two of their granddaughters sang in the girls' ensemble I directed.

"Even though I walk through the darkest valley, I will fear no evil, for you are with me" (Psalm 23:4 NIV).

The following year, after a short illness, his beloved wife died. His heart was broken. He continued faithfully serving God through many assignments at church, but he was praying for God to take him Home too.

Gratefully, God had another plan! He modulated both of our songs into a new key and began to weave them together. We fell in love and were married in 1972; in 1974 God blessed us with a beautiful baby girl. We spent the rest of my husband's life serving God in that wonderful old downtown church. My dear, gentle giant of a husband lived to be ninety-nine years, five months, and three days.

Our sovereign Lord God's beautiful song continues throughout eternity. Where is God leading you? Are you praying, playing, and singing His song, in His key? There is no more beautiful music!

Sing to the LORD a new song;
    sing to the LORD, all the earth.
Sing to the LORD, praise his name;

proclaim his salvation day after day.
Declare his glory among the nations,
his marvelous deeds among all peoples.
For great is the Lord and most worthy of praise.
(Psalm 96:1–4 NIV)

Yudith Cavazos Cruz

YUDITH CAVAZOS CRUZ grew up in deep South Texas as the daughter of ministers. She grew up serving her church, assisting her parents in their various ministries, and translating for mission teams working in the Rio Grande Valley. Yudith's worldview was greatly influenced by her early service with mission teams. As she witnessed the poverty and the need in the border region, a desire to serve the suffering, especially the children, grew deep within her.

With a master's in nursing administration, she is a pediatric nurse and a pediatric nurse educator. She has served as a clinical instructor for the University of Texas Arlington. Yudith moves with ease culturally, linguistically, and with great understanding of the cultures where she works and serves. She and her devoted husband, Jesús, are active church members and enjoy parenting their two beautiful young daughters.

In a Coma for Nine Days

IT WAS NOVEMBER, and we were returning home from my sister-in-law's baby shower. My oldest sister, Mayra, was driving our suburban with my mom and my aunt Maria beside her in the front seat. I sat in the seat directly behind Mayra with my aunt Esperanza and cousin Deyanira. Coming from a Hispanic culture, having an event meant a gathering for many family members.

As we laughed and reflected on the event, we were hit head on by a drunk driver who was driving at fifty-five miles per hour. Even though we were at a complete stop, the impact forced the suburban back several feet. I remember right after the impact asking my mom if she was okay. My next memory was waking up in a hospital bed.

I remember opening my eyes. The first people I saw were Grandma and Dad. Mom, with a cast on her right arm and abrasions on her forehead, came into the hospital room a few minutes later. Dad asked me how I felt, and I remember answering him that I was fine. But I also remember being so confused.

Dad explained to me that we had been in a car accident and that I had been in a coma for nine days. Being so young, I had no knowledge of what a coma was. So, I asked what a coma was and why I had one. Dad explained that I had a skull fracture due to the accident. He went on to tell me that at first, they thought surgery might be needed, but the surgeon later told my parents surgery would not be necessary because I was growing and my bones would fuse together. He also explained the swelling in the brain caused the coma, a deep sleep while my brain was healing.

With my questions answered and my confusion clearing, I asked about my sister, my aunts, and cousin. I learned Mayra had a broken left foot, was in a cast, and was using crutches to walk. Aunt Maria also had a broken right foot and was on crutches. Aunt Esperanza and cousin Deyanira only had abrasions on their arms.

I did not like the fact that my mom had a broken arm and injuries to her face. As one so young, I thought that nothing bad could ever happen to my mom. I did not want her to be in pain.

Two nurses came in while Dad and I were conversing and got me out of bed. My legs were so weak and unsteady as I tried to walk. The nurses explained that it was because I had been in bed for nine days. But they assured me I would get my strength back. They were right. By the next day, I was walking much better and did not want any help. I showered and saw myself in the restroom mirror for the first time. Even after nine days, I still had contusions around my left eye. Mom explained that it was from my head hitting something upon impact when the cars collided. I remember being relieved when she told me it would go away, but I have no memory of what my head struck.

Three days after I woke up from the coma, I was discharged to return home. The discharge had taken so long, and we were all hungry. Dad decided on a treat. So, on the drive home, we stopped at a McDonald's. As we ate, Dad told me that many people had been praying for me for days. I can still see my dad sitting there as we ate our burgers and quoting the scripture that a pastor had shared with him while I was in the coma: "Even when I walk through the darkest valley, I will not be afraid, for you are close beside me. Your rod and your staff protect and comfort me" (Psalm 23:4 NLT).

I recall asking my dad for the first time about the person who hit us in the accident. Dad's face was somber, and he became quiet. Then Dad told me that the man had died instantly. As a young girl, I had no words. My mom's hug said all that could be said.

Dad never told me this directly in our private conversations, but I have heard him share this experience with others. He was so afraid I would die. Now that I am a mother, I fully understand what my parents must have been feeling with their nine-year-old daughter lying in a coma for nine days.

I am thankful to God because in His grace and mercy He allowed me to live. He answered the prayers of those praying for me. I understood that God had a purpose for my life. My defining moment taught me that God has control of everything. My parents' faith was strengthened because of this experience, and the following year at ten years of age, I accepted Jesus Christ as my Savior. At age eleven years, I decided to follow the next step of faith, which was baptism, my public statement that I belong to Jesus and He belongs to me. I am grateful because even in difficult times and in uncertainty, God is present, always with us.

Peace That Surpasses All Understanding

My husband and I were so happy, looking forward to the arrival of our second baby, a son to join his older sister. But things changed quickly. Everything happened so suddenly and too soon. I began to have contractions, and my husband took me to the hospital. There I learned I was already dilated eight centimeters and I would need an emergency cesarean section.

Our son, Santiago, was born at six months and was fine, active, and stable. He was intubated to help his lungs, which were not fully developed. On the second day, Santiago began to show symptoms of infection and became critical. The neonatologist explained to us the complications that could happen when babies are born this premature. Among the possible complications were that the arteries of his brain were so thin they could burst.

When Santiago became critical two days after birth, my husband and I felt as if God had abandoned us and our baby. We prayed earnestly, but Santiago did not show signs of improvement. On the fourth day of his birth, the neonatologist told us he could die and advised us to call the pastor to pray for him, which we did. Santiago remained in critical condition for many days.

Early every morning I arrived at the hospital and spoke to the neonatologist. There was no encouraging news. But in everything, as I listened to the doctors, I would think to myself, and hope and pray, "God, I know you can heal him despite what the doctors say."

Santiago was in such a critical condition that his entire body was swollen. His kidneys shut down, and he was not voiding, and he had many seizures due to the severe infection. He was maxed out on the medications he could receive to help him. It became just a matter of waiting. My days and nights were a constant flow of tears and longing for my son. Every day Santiago was in the hospital was of another day of constant worry.

My husband and I wondered what was going to happen to our precious baby boy. At one point, there was slight improvement in Santiago, which replenished our hope. But our hope was short lived when the infection became so strong the arteries in his brain ruptured, causing the blood in his brain not to flow adequately. At this point, the doctor recommended transferring our baby to a hospital five hours away where a neurosurgeon could evaluate him. A medical flight was arranged for Santiago and me, and my husband and daughter drove to meet us.

More days of waiting and praying, this time in unfamiliar surroundings. Each time I prayed for our son Santiago, I prayed for God to heal him. When I saw no improvement, I would question myself and wonder if I was not praying right. Honestly, we questioned God and why He would allow such to happen to this innocent baby and to us, who loved and served Him. My husband and I prayed and read the Bible together. I remember reading from the Psalms, and my heart resonated with David's heart cries: "Will he never show his favor again? Has his unfailing love vanished forever? Has his promise failed for all time? Has God forgotten to be merciful? Has he in anger withheld his compassion?" (Psalm 77:7–9 NIV)

But we were compelled to continue reading in the same psalm: "I will consider all your works and meditate on all your mighty deeds" (Psalm 77:12 NIV). God's Word was comforting and was what we needed. My husband and I also read together Psalm 73: "My flesh and my heart may fail, but God is the strength of my heart and my portion forever" (Psalm 73:26 NIV).

These psalms describe very well how we felt as we cried out to God on behalf of our son, asking why God would not choose to heal him. We knew that God could heal Santiago the way he healed the blind man and the paralyzed man and raised Lazarus and parted the Red Sea so the Israelites could walk across on dry land. But these same psalms also reminded us that God was with us in this difficult time. I continued to pray for God to heal my son, but I also understood that I should pray for God's will to be done.

On the third day in San Antonio, God showed us what would happen. God was preparing us. It happened in the following manner. In Santiago's hospital room, as the doctor was giving us the MRI results, the monitors connected to our son started to alarm for the first time, indicating his heart rate was very low. The doctor informed us that Santiago had a grade IV brain bleed.

The next day was Sunday. I woke up to pump my breastmilk, and I prayed after pumping. After I finished praying, I felt peace, but I also knew somewhere deep within my soul that Santiago was not going to live much longer on this earth. A few seconds after I finished praying, the phone rang. It was the doctor, calling to inform us that Santiago was critical again. After hanging up, I wept. My husband and I prayed together, got ready quickly, and immediately left for the hospital to see our son.

During the week, we continued to see that our son's heart rate would drop way below normal constantly; his oxygen saturation would drop. His stomach was distended, and he never really could tolerate my breastmilk. These things helped to confirm my sense that Santiago would not be with us much longer.

The doctors called us to inform us that they needed to have a conference to discuss Santiago's condition. During this conference, we were told Santiago's brain tissue was dead due to the bleeding. In the most compassionate way, the doctors suggested for us to consider disconnecting him from all the equipment keeping him alive. After praying and seeking advice, my husband and I felt God's peace and made the decision to disconnect our son and allow him to return peacefully to the One who made him. After he was extubated and removed from all monitors, we held our son in our arms until he gave his last breath. In this process, we felt peace, and we knew that it was from God. We knew that God was holding us just as He was holding our infant Santiago.

We know God is sovereign and He is good. Our son's death still hurts us. We had such hopes for him and were so excited to have him join our family. We named him *Santiago,* which means "a gift from God" or "of St. James." We are thankful to God for the month of life He allowed our son to live. God has comforted us and continues to do so. We are comforted in the hope we have in Him that we will see our son Santiago again.

On the day of Santiago's memorial service, I was so comforted by this passage read by the pastor: "The secret things belong to the Lord our God, but the things revealed belong to us and to our children forever, that we may follow all the words of this law" (Deuteronomy 29:29 NIV). There are things we do not and are not meant to understand, but this I know: I trust God. I love my Lord and Savior, and I know that His will is good, pleasing, and perfect. God has not allowed my pain to be wasted. In my job as a nurse, I minister to those who are suffering in a much deeper way of understanding and with more compassion because of my own pain, loss, and sorrow.

Dr. Jim Denison

Jim Denison, PhD, is an author, speaker, and the CEO of Denison Ministries, which is transforming 6.8 million lives through meaningful digital content. Dallas-based Denison Ministries includes DenisonForum.org, First15.org, ChristianParenting.org, and FoundationsWithJanet.org.

Dr. Denison speaks biblically into significant cultural issues at DenisonForum.org and DrJimDenison.com, as well as on radio, TV, podcasts, and social media. Dr. Denison speaks multiple times per year at events, seminars, and churches and is a frequent guest on radio and television programs.

He is the author of over thirty books, including:

- *The Coming Tsunami: Why Christians Are Labeled Intolerant, Irrelevant, Oppressive, and Dangerous—and How We Can Turn the Tide*
- *Respectfully, I Disagree: How to Be a Civil Person in an Uncivil Time*
- Biblical Insight to Tough Questions series, a ten-volume set

He has taught the philosophy of religion and apologetics at several seminaries. Dr. Denison serves as resident scholar for ethics with Baylor Scott & White Health, where he addresses issues such as genetic medicine and reproductive science. He is a senior fellow with CEO Forum, 21st Century Wilberforce Initiative, International Alliance of Christian Education, and Dallas Baptist University's Institute for Global Engagement.

He holds a doctor of philosophy and a master of divinity degree from Southwestern Baptist Theological Seminary. He also received an honorary doctor of divinity from Dallas Baptist University. Dr. Denison is the theologian in residence for the Baptist General Convention of Texas. Prior to launching Denison Forum in 2009, he pastored churches in Texas and Georgia.

Jim and his wife, Janet, live in Dallas, Texas. They have two married sons and four grandchildren.

The First Person I Baptized in Cuba

I TELL THE following story often because it left an indelible mark on my life.

I've served in Cuba many times over the years, and I've been grateful to do so. If you've never been, allow me to set a brief context for the lives of our Cuban Christian brothers and sisters.

Decades ago, I recorded that the average monthly salary in Cuba was $7. If you made $30, you earned an excellent salary. Yet things cost as much there as here: at that time, a bottle of water was $1.30, and I saw shoes for sale for $140. (Today, inflation is in the double digits as a result of the pandemic and the worsening political environment. Cubans are also suffering from a severe shortage of food and basic necessities. In many ways, their environment is reminiscent of our Great Depression in the 1930s.)

When I visited, the Cubans we met depended on the rice and beans given by the government, worked two or three jobs, and bartered with each other for goods and services they needed. They ate chicken once a month and beef once a year.

So, imagine our surprise at the meals they served us: fried chicken, ham, beef, even lobster. Wonderful banquets, each one. What if our team had sat down to such sacrificial meals with boredom, ate little or nothing, and took for granted such gifts?

Trust me, we did not. We ate each such meal with enormous gratitude for their sacrifice and love. That's just one example of multitudes of the kinds of grace we received when visiting Christians in Cuba.

I believe it was providential that we were fed so well. We needed the energy for Sunday-morning worship services, which often began at 9:00 a.m. and ended at 12:50 p.m. The exuberance of their worship and their faith was thrilling. In the midst of oppressive poverty and governmental control, their joy in Jesus was contagious.

Mother Teresa said, "You'll never know that Jesus is all you need until Jesus is all you have." They have only Jesus. And he's enough.

Their faith was visible, tangible, and infectious. That was never more apparent to me than on one particular occasion.

An Unforgettable Experience

The first person I baptized in Cuba was a woman whose name I do not know but whose faith I cannot forget.

On one of our mission trips, the pastor of our partner church announced on Sunday morning that there would be a mass baptism service after worship services. This was a momentous announcement.

In Cuban evangelical churches, baptism is a major

step and risk. When a person is baptized publicly, government informants record their names. These believers can lose their jobs or homes; their children can be sent to the worst schools or given the worst military assignments. As a result, Cuban churches typically require months of discipleship training before new converts are allowed to be baptized. Their goal is to prepare these believers for the persecution they will soon face.

On this Sunday, so many people were ready for baptism that the pastor needed help. So he asked me and the other members of our team if we would help him baptize. What a great privilege. He taught us the baptismal formula in Spanish as we prepared for an experience unlike any we had seen.

Then the massive congregation traveled to a shallow lake outside town where they typically conduct their mass baptisms. The pastor and our team waded out into the water. The large crowd stood on the shore singing hymns and offering prayers of thanksgiving to God.

When we were ready, those coming for baptism began wading out into the lake.

The first person who came to me, however, was a woman being carried through the water by a man. I learned later that this was her husband. I could see only her head, shoulders, and arms above the water.

I wondered why she had not walked out by herself.

The Joy of the Lord

He handed her to me in the water. I repeated the baptismal formula, lowered her into the water, and raised her back up.

She threw her arms into the air and began shouting, "Alleluia! Alleluia!" Her husband began jumping up and down with joy. Her family on the shore joined their gratitude and worship.

Then, as he took her back into his arms, he raised her out of the water, and I saw that she had only one leg.

Life in Cuba is difficult. Life for believers is harder. Life for a Christian with a disability like hers is beyond my imagination. But if you could have seen the joy in her face that day, you would want whatever she has.

I have so many distinctly fond memories of serving alongside our brothers and sisters in Christ in Cuba, but I will never forget the look of joy on that woman's face as she rose from the waters of baptism.

In recalling that moment, and how grateful our team was for the gracious, sacrificial nature of their dinners for us, I'm reminded that, at baptism, we celebrate Jesus' love for us. Once we are baptized, we ought to continue to live every day as though it were our baptism day—in joy.

When My Oldest Son Had Cancer

RYAN DENISON CHANGED our lives forever when he was born. He and his brother were the greatest gifts Janet and I ever received from the Lord (until our perfect grandchildren came along).

Both men are married to amazing, beautiful, godly women, and both of their families serve the Lord with the gifts and abilities they've been given. We would love to take credit for the men of God they have become, but we know that the Holy Spirit has formed their character far more than their parents.

I used to say that my father's death when I was in college was the most painful experience of my life. Then Ryan was diagnosed with acinic cell carcinoma in January 2012. He quickly underwent surgery that February and endured radiation the following March and April.

A Thorn in Our Flesh

Shortly after his diagnosis, Ryan told me that he was angry with the Lord for allowing this to happen to him, a sentiment I certainly shared. Then he said: "As I prayed about this, I sensed that God wants this to be a 'thorn in the flesh' that he will use to help me trust him more than I would have otherwise." I'll never forget that conversation.

As you may know, the apostle Paul suffered from a "thorn in my flesh" (see 2 Corinthians 12:7). Scholars debate its nature—some think it was malaria, others suggest migraine headaches or failing eyesight (cf. Galatians 6:11 ESV, where Paul states, "See with what large letters I am writing to you with my own hand!").

While we don't know the identity of his "thorn," we do know its result: after Paul prayed three times for God to remove it, he heard the Lord say, "My grace is sufficient for you, for my power is made perfect in weakness" (2 Corinthians 12:9 ESV). The apostle concluded: "Therefore I will boast all the more gladly of my weaknesses, so that the power of Christ may rest upon me. For the sake of Christ, then, I am content with weaknesses, insults, hardships, persecutions, and calamities. For when I am weak, then I am strong." (vv. 9–10 ESV).

Likewise, Ryan is grateful for the ways God has redeemed his cancer. He has learned to rely on the Lord for his future and his health. He and his wife depend on the Father far more than they would have if he had never developed this terrible disease. They are examples to me whenever I become discouraged—if God can redeem cancer, he can redeem anything.

In June 2012, just five months after his diagnosis, Ryan was deemed cancer free, for which we thank God every day.

Living for Eternity

When Janet and I received that news, our first reaction was one of great joy. Upon reflection, however, I wondered if that was the most biblical way we could have responded.

Why did we want Ryan to have many more years of life on this fallen planet? In part, of course, we wanted to spare him the suffering that a recurrence of cancer would bring. But part of our motive was surely selfish—we didn't want to lose him. However, even saying that was indicative of unbiblical thinking. We would not "lose" our son, for you "lose" what you cannot find. We knew he would be in heaven and that we would see him again.

Another part of my motive for desperately wanting Ryan to be healed was that he has so much to offer the kingdom. He's a remarkable theologian even as a young adult (I'm reluctant to brag on him, but it's really true). His mind and heart are truly surrendered to Christ as his King. He and his wife, Candice, would make such a difference in so many lives.

But doesn't God know all of this? If the King chose not to heal his cancer, would he have made a mistake in administering his kingdom?

Early Christians lived every day as if it would be their last and looked forward with great anticipation to the day they would be reunited with their Lord (see 1 Thessalonians 4:15–18). Have we lost their hope in heaven?

The fact is living for eternity is the best way to live today. We make biblical choices when we remember that we'll be held accountable for them. We care about eternal people more than temporal possessions, placing the significant before the urgent. The problems of the day become less burdensome when we know that "this light momentary affliction is preparing for us an eternal weight of glory beyond all comparison" (2 Corinthians 4:17 ESV).

Upon reflection, the biblical emphasis on eternity makes the most sense today.

Early Christians could pray, "Come, Lord Jesus" (see Revelation 22:20). Can you?

Ryan, thankfully, is still cancer free. However, since his type of malignancy can recur many years later, he must continue to get MRIs periodically to check for signs of the cancer's return—a thorn in the flesh, to be sure, but also a constant reminder of God's sovereignty and grace.

Dr. Dean Dickens

FROM THE HILLS of Northwest Arkansas, Dean and his wife, Karr La, have found themselves in changing ministries all their lives. His obedience to the call of God began with him bargaining, "Okay, Lord, I'll preach or do anything you want of me—except please do not call me to overseas missions." Several years into Ouachita Baptist University and Southwestern Baptist Theological Seminary, he and his identical twin brother, Doug, began by copastoring the same church and then doing almost two hundred youth led revivals all over the southwestern United States. While Dean completed his PhD and taught preaching, Doug completed his PhD and taught pastoral care.

Only a few years into teaching preaching at Southwestern Seminary, God did it again: God called Dean and Karr La into global missions, where they served for twenty-eight years. At various intervals, they served in the Philippines as pastor and seminary teachers. Then they served eleven years in metropolitan pastoring in Dallas, Texas. His congregation began twenty-three missions and sponsored a care ministry that fed and clothed over twenty-two thousand people in one year.

Then came another twelve years of supervising field missionaries worldwide. Today he spends his time working with congregations in Intentional Interim Ministry, primarily serving churches who are either in crisis, in limbo, or who have run out of a contemporary mission and vision. In 2020 he was named Texas Baptists' Outstanding Intentional Pastor. He has two books on preaching, both translated in numerous languages. He still does cross-cultural preaching workshops globally.

Reluctant Confession: I Hate Bad Times—But They've Made Me a Better Minister

It's painful for a "Professional Holy Person" to confess it, but I must: I really wish the apostle James had not written, "Consider it pure joy, my brothers, whenever you face trials of many kinds, because you know that the testing of your faith produces perseverance" (James 1:2–3 NIV). On the other hand, I must admit that it is true. The lesson started early with me, yet I remember it as if it was yesterday even though it was over seventy years ago.

My twin brother and I were five, my sister was four, and we had just been "dumped" at the orphanage. I know today that my parents could not help it. Both of them were being confined and treated for tuberculosis, and there simply was no other place we could go than to the Masonic Orphanage at the Arkansas Tuberculosis Sanatorium. I can still see their car drive away as I screamed at them, at the world, and mostly at God. At five years of age, I certainly did not know much about God, but as I threw rock after rock at that old pine tree, I called God every bad name my five-year-old brain could remember. And then the car was gone and they were gone. I wasn't really happy about James' idea of trials helping me. But they did. James was right.

The next six years or so were interesting. For instance, I learned not to expect too much from Christmas and nothing at all from birthdays. The Masonic Lodge was wonderful as they came around twice a year. Perhaps it was a balsa-wood airplane kit. Maybe a cowboy holster and gun. Seventy years later, I still think that the most meaningful birthday present I ever received was a one-dollar Sheaffer Skrip cartridge ink pen my mother somehow managed to buy for me. For our family, that one-dollar pen was authentic sacrificial giving. (For some reason, even after all these years, I have kept one of those cartridges in my office as a reminder.) The "normal" I learned was not to expect too much.

And there were many other "normals" that shaped life and ministry. In our orphanage over those years, girls and boys were kept separate. So, while my identical twin brother, Doug, and I had each other, my sister, Diane, had nobody. This was my seminal understanding of *family*. But James was right: while those days were difficult, those very experiences shaped me into a pastor who understood family trauma and the need for compassionate ministry. Family life today can be tough for people, and they all need encouragement.

Three times daily, we stood in line to get into the cafeteria for meals. It was not uncommon for Nurse Ella to talk (sometimes loudly) to me about what a terrible man my father was. "He's a drunk." (True.) "He's in trouble with the law." (Sometimes true.) "He's not a good man." (Never true.) Over the years, I came to recognize that my father, a man who actually didn't sober up until about age forty-five when he joined Alcoholics Anonymous, was a genuinely good man who cared deeply for others. After spending many years of "religious service" as a missionary, seminary professor, and pastor, I finally understood that while my dad was far from perfect, he spent the rest of his sober life helping other alcoholics get sober and become productive people.

At his funeral, person after person stopped to tell how my "drunk of a father" had changed their lives. One of Dad's best drunk friends had even become a minister. (Over the years, watching drunks rescue drunks has often made me think that perhaps AA does "church" better than most churches. Of course, I must also confess that this opinion has not always endeared me to overly sensitive church leaders.) But I've come to recognize, particularly as I preach, that for most people in and out of our churches, life is tough and people need encouragement. I came to understand that my marine corps father, shot through the jaws and left for dead on the beaches of Guadalcanal, needed whatever he could get to dull pain and life. And his experience made me a better minister and a more empathetic minister. James was right: without that trauma, this pastor would never have developed a listening ear instead of a judgmental heart.

Since my twin brother, Doug, and I are both engaged in Christian ministry, I am often asked, "So how did you become involved with the church?" Understandably, there was no church at the orphanage. Fortunately, there were fine Christian men and women who regularly visited and became "church" to us on Sundays. Every month came Baptist minister Charles Finch, followed by Methodist minister Bates Sturdy and by Church of Christ minister Howard Casada. The fourth Sunday we were blessed with Catholic priest Father George Vianni. Interestingly enough, the diverse theology of these men did not confuse me about theology because each man, living out his own theology, provided a razor-sharp image of how very much God loved boys and girls in an orphanage. Following in their footsteps, I determined to give my best in sharing God's great love with others. I could not have done it without these fine men joining my own "trials of many kinds." Again, reluctantly, I confess that James got it right.

Finally, there was my beloved mother dying young at age fifty-nine. She carried the load for our family. While Dad was often out, Mom was the "stay-at-home-dad-and-mom" who cooked, cleaned, dressed, got us off to school, and even rode the bus with us to church. The pressures and strain in raising three teenagers while dealing with what we today might call bipolar issues put our mother in the state mental hospital twice. But each time she came out even more determined to make our lives count.

Little could she know that she herself was God's minister to two soon-to-be ministers. How impressive to me one revival meeting night was her simple statement to our pastor that "I have come forward to say that I want my children to know that I love the Lord." Not long before she died, she told my pastor/seminary professor brother, "Do not ever give up on your father." She didn't.

We didn't. And, thankfully, God didn't.

That loving persistence has framed almost sixty years of my ministry. It wasn't taught in seminary textbooks. It was taught in the hardships of life as God interpreted James's statement to me. If I were scripting my life, would I have written these things into it? Absolutely not. But I would never trade what these "trials" taught me. James was right. Those hardships shaped my life and ministry.

Over a century ago, American poet Robert Browning Hamilton in his poem "Along the Road" said it just about as well as the apostle James.

> I walked a mile with Pleasure;
> She chatted all the way;
> But left me none the wiser
> For all she had to say.
>
> I walked a mile with Sorrow;
> And ne'er a word said she;
> But, oh! The things I learned from her,
> When Sorrow walked with me.

A "Too Busy" Servant of God

I REMEMBER EXACTLY when the reality hit me. And it was painful.

The place was Kota Kinabalu, Malaysia, and I was starting another workshop for beginning Asian preachers. Since the Philippine Baptist Theological Seminary and our Asia Baptist Graduate School of Theology had just finished, I had eight whole weeks before school began again. Unwisely, I scheduled all those weeks with international workshops. Now, sitting in that hotel room, I was already homesick. Setting out the pictures of my wife, Karr La, and our three children, I just stared and reflected, counting over and over how many years each child had left before leaving home for college in the United States.

Then God hit me with one of those Defining Moments: "You're too busy. And you're not even busy about the right things."

I was shocked. God had called me to this. God had led us to Global Missions in Asia. "But I like being busy. And besides, this work is for You. I am Your servant. I'm Your missionary." But that nagging, still, small voice just couldn't leave it alone. So, I began to do an "honest-to-God" checklist.

First, I had just been asked if I would serve as the president of our seminary while the long-term president took his furlough stateside. It was a privilege. In addition, I was teaching a full load of preaching classes. Third, I was teaching a doctoral preaching seminar to graduate students. Fourth, I was serving as the secretary for our Asian Baptist Graduate School of Theology consortium of schools. I edited the *Journal of Preaching*, which came out twice a year. Additionally, Karr La and I had just begun a new congregation meeting at the local Hyatt Hotel and were focusing on our city's professional community. Seventh, I was doing numerous cross-cultural preaching workshops all over Asia, helping beginning preachers (many of whom had only a Bible) learn how to study and formulate sermon forms appropriate to their specific cultures. I loved it. Adding to that, I was the "Luzon Island Chairman" of our one hundred missionaries (dealing with job descriptions, housing, budgets, personnel issues, and mission relationships with the local Baptist associations and conventions). Yep! I loved it too. I was also on our mission administrative committee helping guide the mission. Finally, I was involved in the Rotary Club with local businessmen, political leaders, and others.

Even reading the list today makes me shudder. I was one busy servant of God.

And then God began to push harder in this Defining Moment. "Don't you think, if you are really concerned about your family, that you should pay attention to this now rather than waiting to grieve after they are gone?"

And then, in that irritating way that God sometimes has: "What is important and what should you give up so that you can give Me what I want?"

I came home from Malaysia and sat down with my wife to talk with her about what had just happened and what decisions I felt led to make. She very graciously said, "Well, that's probably a good thing. While you were gone, our son Douglas asked one night at supper, 'Is Daddy going to live with us again?'"

As I began to cull activities so I could focus on my family and my calling to this teaching ministry, I stumbled across a scripture passage that had haunted me for years. In 1 Kings chapter 20 is the intriguing story of God entrusting Israel's (evil) King Ahab with a victory over the overwhelming military forces of the blasphemous King Ben-Hadad. In the account, one of God's prophets confronted King Ahab about being so busy with "things" that he ignored God's task. Having been told to guard a prisoner at the cost of losing his life, he was so busy, he failed at the one thing he was asked to do. The servant's excuse was damning and convicting: "While your servant was busy here and there, the man disappeared" (v. 40 NIV). It was not difficult for me to determine that, while I had been God's servant committed to God's ministries, I had often found myself stymied, worn out, and frustrated because "your servant was busy here and there."

I wish it was possible to acknowledge that, having had this Defining Moment, my ministry has remained focused and clear. Unfortunately, I discovered that this was not a lifetime decision but was one that needed to be reaffirmed over and over. When, after sixteen years, God led us from the Philippines to an urban pastorate, I found it easy to go back to my natural workaholic mentality. I loved the church. I loved the people. I loved pastoring. I loved preaching. I loved hospital visitation. I loved pastoral visiting. I loved it all. So, on automatic pilot, I went two years without taking a vacation or a day off. I loved it…until I didn't love it. Tired, exhausted, angry, "your servant was busy here and there." Sometimes these Defining Moments need to be revisited and renewed over and over again.

Today, blessed with good health even after almost sixty years of ministry, "your servant [who is often] busy here and there" has come (finally?) to develop a few insights about times when God's servant slips back into being a "too busy" servant of God. None of them are new, nor are any original, but they have guided me, and perhaps they can guide that God's servant called "you":

1. Figure out what is the Main Thing and keep the Main Thing as the Main Thing.
2. Do not allow the "tyranny of the urgent" to keep you from that which is your priority.
3. Don't be so quick to choose the "good" or the "better" that you fail to wait for the "best."

Kota Kinabalu was not a wonderful moment. But it was a Defining Moment.

Karr La Dickens

Karr La Dickens is retired, living in the Dallas, TX, area since 1989. She and her husband, Dean, have three grown children and three grandchildren. She has her music degree from Ouachita Baptist University and taught music in Texas public schools for fourteen years, particularly loving the use of the Orff-Schulwerk methods in her classrooms. The PTA awarded her a lifetime membership for her work in classrooms and choirs.

The Dickens have served with two missionary organizations: the International Mission Board as field personnel in the Philippines and the Cooperative Baptist Fellowship Global Missions in a supervisory role. In her role as a missionary, she had many varied experiences, including representative to the United Nations DPI-

NGO, Red Cross volunteer on Clark Field Air Base as a water safety instructor, accompanying the Fil-Am choir at Clark Field Baptist Church for a Billy Graham Team, and singing as a soloist for Handel's *Messiah* accompanied by the Air Force Band of the Pacific at the Philippine Cultural Center in Manila.

But best of all were the relationships with people all over the world and watching today as her former students from the Philippine Baptist Theological Seminary assume leadership positions in Asia and in US ministries.

A Picture

MANY PEOPLE EXPRESS confusion about knowing God's plan for one's life. Our creative God speaks to people in many different ways. For me, it was an accumulation of decisions I made with a particular picture in mind. Let me tell you about that picture and one major decision.

I was eight years old when I walked into the back bedroom of the parsonage where we lived and saw my daddy sitting on the edge of the bed staring out of the windows at the forest of pine trees in our back yard, crying. I had never seen my daddy cry before. I tiptoed back into the kitchen and asked Mother, "Why is Daddy crying?"

She said, "He is sad because God wants him to go to another church, and he had to tell our church that he has to follow God's call."

I learned over the following years that Dad's decision to move from Bauxite Baptist Church in Bauxite, Arkansas, to First Baptist Church in Mena, Arkansas, was indeed an incredibly hard decision. His fellow pastors and convention leaders from across the state had been calling him, encouraging him *not* to go to Mena. The year was 1956, and it seems that the church was in big trouble! They were so broke the convention's Sunday school department would not even send them the quarterly lesson books!

Now, in Baptist life, that is really broke! But God was telling my Dad to go. It was one of the hardest decisions he ever made. I saw the tears of struggle and that picture still stays with me—a defining moment. Dad obeyed and pastored that church for twenty-eight years.

So, is it any wonder that when I've had to make a potentially life-changing decision, the influence of that picture has been in my mind? Here is one example of how that picture affected my future career choices: I was a music education major at Ouachita Baptist University. My primary study was voice, and my secondary was piano. My voice teacher, Mr. David Scott, had entered me in a voice competition sponsored by the Arkansas Chapter of the National Federation of Music Educators. I won first place in the state competition, and then second place in the three-state district competition. (The winner of the district competition had a chance of an audition with the Metropolitan Opera in New York City.) Placing second was fine with me because I had another dream. I dreamed of being a summer missionary with the Baptist Home Mission Board.

So, Mr. Scott called me into his office one fine spring afternoon. He was so excited because the Music Federation wanted to honor me with a scholarship to Inspiration Point, a summer-long opera workshop. Interestingly enough, the same week I received an acceptance letter from the Home Mission Board to spend the summer working with Baptist churches in Wisconsin.

I had a decision to make: The workshop would put me on track to NYC and opera. The mission program would put me on track for discovering a calling to career missions.

Mr. Scott thought it was a no-brainer, but I had been feeling led towards mission work since I was a little girl. A looming decision ahead—a defining moment! Thinking about living my life going from one audition to another wasn't what I wanted to do. Missions was not only a natural choice for me, but also what I felt I needed to be about. And oh, boy, explaining that to Mr. Scott wasn't a pretty picture. He was livid, and the rest of the music faculty was very disappointed in me. After all, I was the very first student who had ever been offered a scholarship to Inspiration Point by the Federation.

But that picture of Daddy was there in my mind. "Do what you feel God is leading you to do. It may not be easy, and you may disappoint some people, but it is the best way." I cried too. But I never looked back. Missions was my call, and music was my work within that calling.

Here are wise words from a wise man who knew something about life: "Listen for GOD's voice in everything you do, everywhere you go; he's the one who will keep you on track" (Proverbs 3:6 MSG).

Epilogue

OUR DAUGHTER COURTNEY happens to look like me. And she was a student at Ouachita about thirty years after I graduated. She told me that she was in the music building one afternoon when a professor walked by her and did a double take. He said, "You must be Karr La Miller's daughter."

She answered, "Yes, I am."

He said, "Yeah, she was supposed to go to New York City..."

God had a different plan.

Who's Calling?

"Hello?"

"Yes, hello. Is this Mrs. Dickens?"

"Yes, it is."

"Mrs. Dickens, my name is Keith Parks. I work for the Foreign Mission Board. May I speak with your husband?"

Gulp! A defining moment!

That's how it all began! I often laugh, telling Keith that *he* called us to the mission field. He just rolls his eyes and says, "Oh, Karr La. You know that isn't so!"

Really, it all began long before the phone call, almost twenty-five years earlier in 1945. I'll explain: Dean and I were in our first year of marriage and living in Fort Worth, Texas, when Dr. Parks called us. The Manila International Baptist Church needed an interim pastor to serve there while the regular pastor was on a year's furlough. The church had a large youth group made up mostly of MKs (missionary kids). So they were asking if a young pastor could come and serve for the year rather than the usual older retirees. Dean's name had been given to Keith by several professors at the seminary. Would we be willing to go?

Dean told Dr. Parks no because he had just been accepted into the seminary's PhD program, and I had secured a good teaching position. Then Dean added, "*But—*" Uh-oh. "—if you can't find anyone else, let me know, and we will talk again." Dean hung up the phone and turned to me and said, "Don't worry. He will find someone else. Who wouldn't want to go?" And we didn't think about it anymore.

A few weeks later, Dr. Parks called again. He said he had not been able to find anyone, and he would really like to visit with us. He lived in Richmond, Virginia, but his mother lived in Danville, Arkansas, just down the road from Dean's home in Booneville. Would we be willing to meet him at Dean's home over the July Fourth weekend? We agreed. So he came and talked with us about the church, which was full of missionary families, US Embassy personnel, and Filipino professionals. He talked about the logistics of living in Manila, and before we knew it, we had agreed that we could, after all, put our lives "on hold" for a year and move to the Philippines.

Now for the backstory: I grew up in Mena, Arkansas, and my dad was the pastor of the First Baptist Church. He was a very mission-minded pastor. The James Hampton family in East Africa was from our church, and it was always an exciting day when James would call Dad from New York City to say, "We have landed in the US for our year's furlough! See you soon!" That happened every four years. Those were precious times with the Hampton family. I was so impressed by the missionaries!

Our church also had summer missionaries—college students who used their summer vacation to work in various mission projects. They were always in and out of our home and were so much fun! And our church had a strong Royal Ambassador program for the boys and Girls Auxiliary for the girls. There we were taught about various ministries of our convention and learned a lot about mission work around the world. Interestingly enough, at the same time, a young teenage boy in Booneville's First Baptist Church was struggling with a call to preach. He prayed one night, "Okay, Lord, I'll be a preacher. Just don't send me to China!"

So, it happened. Dean and I got our passports and required inoculations, and off we went to Manila, Philippines! Just for a year…

It seems that this wasn't just a defining moment, it was a defining year! We loved being part of the entire missionary community—and not just the Baptists. The church's minister of music was a Quaker! The Cadd family remained our friends for decades. The friendships we built with Filipino friends were priceless. We fell in love with a country, with a culture, with a mission.

And then we grieved to leave our friends and the mission family when our year came to an end. We returned to Fort Worth, where Dean completed his PhD, and I returned to teaching music in the public schools.

While still in seminary, Dean and I went to Glorieta, New Mexico, for a week-long church retreat. The focus for that week was overseas mission work. At that retreat, we both felt that God was calling us to be missionaries.

We applied and were accepted by the Foreign Mission Board (now the International Mission Board) of the Southern Baptist Convention.

Even more backstory—the year was 1974. So, what's the deal about my going back to 1945? Well, my parents were students at Ouachita Baptist College from 1942 to 1945. Daddy chose that Baptist college because he knew God was calling him to be a pastor.

Now, thirty years later, Dean and I were being commissioned in Little Rock, Arkansas, to be missionaries in the Philippines. My mother came to our hotel room before the commissioning service to bring me a new dress to wear. Then she told me something that was breathtaking. She told me that while she and Daddy were students at Ouachita, they attended chapel services during Foreign Missions Week, and they both felt strongly that they were being called to foreign mission work. But why? God knew that the board would never appoint them as missionaries because Daddy had a heart issue that would never pass the rigid physical exams. But they went to the altar at the front during the invitation time to commit themselves to missions. Mother looked me in the eye and said, "The Lord called us so you would go!"

I was born two years after that defining moment—a generational defining moment. A few years later, First Baptist Church of Mena was recognized at the annual Baptist Convention because even though they were only a church of 250 people, it had sent out five families into mission work!

Who's calling? God is calling!
Isaiah said it well:

"And then I heard the voice of the Master:
'Whom shall I send?
Who will go for us?'

I spoke up,
'I'll go.
Send me!'" (Isaiah 6:8 MSG)

Linda Hibner

LINDA HIBNER HAS devoted her life to being an advocate for children after realizing the crucial impact we can have on early development. For over thirty years, she has served in various capacities including minister to preschoolers, minister of weekday education, and children's center director at several Texas churches including Houston First Baptist Church and Southwestern Baptist Theological Seminary.

She is one of the cofounders of One by One Ministries, a parenting mentoring program for expectant and new parents based in Memphis, Tennessee. She also served as the first program director for One by One and wrote the curriculum used by the ministry.

Linda has been a keynote speaker, conference leader,

and trainer for national and state denominational conventions and early-education agencies. She has also written Sunday school curriculum.

Taking Grace Home is Linda's book in progress. It is a women's Bible study/devotional book exploring the discoveries, opportunities, and adventures of a reimagined, re-joyed, and redeemed homestretch.

Linda currently is a GriefShare ministry leader, ladies' Bible study teacher, and host of a monthly small group using material from *Taking Grace Home,* her book in progress. She enjoys art quilting, paper arts, journaling, working on Christmas year-round, and spending time with her family.

Website: lindajhibner.com (blog launching in June 2022)
Facebook: Linda Hibner

Evidence of Grace

Flirting with my husband was always my favorite activity. All I had to do was call Russ Handsome Dude for his cute, impish grin to appear. It sometimes surprised us that we loved each other so much. Because God kept working on us, we kissed, fought, talked, and laughed our way through nearly fifty-four years of marriage.

We danced in the kitchen or anywhere music was playing. Russ was a good dancer, and I was an enthusiastic one with two left feet. Once I begged Russ to try a move we'd seen on television. Without warning, he dramatically tossed me backward and immediately lost his grip on my back. With a loud thud I landed on the floor with Russ tumbling after me. It took us forever to get up because we were laughing so hard. We loved telling this story that was so us!

While our personalities and gifts were different, we shared the same life goal to serve the Lord. We did ministry together and prayed for each other. We were a team in every sense of the word. The life we created together wasn't perfect, but it sure was good and full of evidence of God's love and grace.

Then came that day in 2020 when our good life was

blindsided by Acute Myeloid Leukemia, an insidious adult cancer. It was a fierce eighteen-day battle from the first afternoon Russ felt ill to the early morning of July 07, 2020, when he took his last breath and woke up with Jesus, totally healed.

Russ got heaven, and I got a trajectory change that landed me on what seemed like the far side of the moon. Nothing felt right or familiar. I decided that feeling a little disoriented in those first horrendous moments of grief wasn't such a bad thing.

Somehow, the next few days went by. There were calls to make, people to notify, and memorial plans to prepare. The mornings after Russ's homegoing found me using tools I had discovered years before—journaling and keeping a blessing/gratitude jar. My condensed journal entry for July 09, 2020:

> Another morning—not so scary. Time passes as it always does. The atmosphere around me varies from the closeness of You, Father, to the deep crying out and hurt of not having Russ. I ask for forgiveness when I let the grief overpower me. Already this morning there are seven gratitude slips written! Every slip reassures me You are showing up. So many blessings You've given me—Your presence and comfort being top of the list. Father, there are moments that seem as normal as my old life. There are, of course, those moments when I absolutely fall apart. Without You, there would be no hope. Russ was my earthly partner, such a huge part of my life. Yet I know

> that You are my God, Father, Comforter... It's hard for me to say, but this is my new life... There is a future, though I find it hard to see. I will survive and thrive but not the way I had planned.

Amazingly, two days after Russ's homegoing, the Lord gave me the first version of my defining moment, which would accelerate my grief recovery and help my transition from wife to widow. "There is a future... I will survive and thrive." I didn't recognize this as a defining moment yet, but I grabbed the thought anyway and clung to it! Like every other grace gift, I didn't earn this confirmation or deserve it, but here it was.

By July 13 I had looked at my finances and made the monumental decision, with the help of a good friend and financial advisor, to sell our house and move closer to one of my daughters. I received instant criticism from another widow for making such a big decision so early in my grief recovery. I did the bravest thing I think I've ever done. I smiled and made no reply. Whether or not anyone approved, I was now in charge of my life, and only I knew what my needs were. It was a powerful moment.

As I prepared to list my house, I needed to clean the large prayer garden Russ had designed for me. Just being in the space where Russ had spent so much time creating such beauty brought a flood of tears. Between the backdraft of the leaf blower, the hot sun, and my crying, I was soon covered in dirt streaked by my perspiration and my tears. With my nose running and mud forming around my eyes, I wiped my face with my very dirty shirt sleeve. That only smeared the dirt into the wet tear streaks on my face. Everything I tried to do after that became a comedy of errors. I started laughing and couldn't stop. It hit me that if I could have a funny moment all by myself, I was going to be all right. In that crazy moment of tears and laughter, hope rose in me that I had a future that still included joy.

On September 07, 2020, three months after Russ' homegoing, I journaled:

> I will remember forever, Lord, how You've carried me through the last ninety impossible days. Here's the truth I hold onto: "Your eyes saw my unformed body; all the days ordained for me were written in your book before one of them came to be" (Psalm 139:16 NIV). Your sovereignty and goodness keep me believing that if You planned so well for Russ, You have a plan for me. I won't accept that my purpose is just being Russ's grieving widow.

I completed the sale of the home that I had shared with Russ and bought a house in another town close to one of my daughters. Once I got moved into my new house, I could stop the frenzied activity the move had generated. I took the next several months to stay home and unpack and decorate. I registered for GriefShare, a Christian grief recovery program. I started concentrating on completing the healing journey that I had started months ago when the Lord had assured me I had a future.

In the last twenty-two-plus months, I've developed some perspective on the impact of Russ's homegoing and my defining moment. The first lesson I learned was that as much as Russ and I loved each other and lived our lives in tandem, we each belonged individually to God first. He had brought us together, and we truly became one in every sense of the word. However, the Lord's purpose and plans for us were always individual ones.

A final lesson I learned was to take God at His word, believe His promises, and hold on to hope. "'For I know the plans I have for you,' declares the LORD, 'plans to prosper you and not to harm you, plans to give you hope and a future'" (Jeremiah 29:11 NIV).

Destinations

LIFE-ALTERING OPPORTUNITIES OUGHT to come with warnings: Guaranteed to Turn Your Life Upside Down/Inside Out! Not for the Faint Hearted!

Nearly forty years ago a large Christian family services agency offered my husband, Russ, and me an opportunity that at first glance wasn't very appealing to us. When we shared the news with family and friends, their response was, "They want you to do what?!"

We were asked to consider becoming house parents for one of the agency's group foster homes. Little did we know that this opportunity would come to define the next eight years of our lives and end up influencing the career paths for every member of our family.

We were ready to refuse this agency's offer based on our negative experience with another smaller family services agency. However, we felt it only fair to pray and talk with our daughters, who were ten and fourteen at the time. Our concerns were having to move to a small town sixty miles away and Russ having to quit his job, one he loved. He and I would have identical positions, neither of which offered the salary, advancement opportunities, or benefits of Russ's current job. For our daughters it meant changing schools and living in a house with eight to ten other children.

We were shocked when after lengthy discussions, all of us agreed that this sounded like a ministry adventure that would be good for our family. Looking back, I recognize that signing the agency's employee forms was a defining moment. It changed not just our address but also gave us a destination where our whole family flourished. We were also setting off for our new life with the least amount of financial security with which we'd ever lived.

We moved into the group foster home in May of 1981 to begin this challenging and rewarding time of our lives. Over the next eight years we provided care for six to eight residents at a time, ranging in age from six to seventeen years. The majority of the residents stayed with us from six months to four years and came from every ethnicity and economic background.

To handle the day-to-day complications and challenges of a household of up to twelve people, Russ and I organized every facet of our lives. Everyone had chores, and we did them daily. We mixed our furniture with what was already in the foster home to make the nearly 4,500-square-foot house feel like a warm and inviting place. We served sit-down meals with required attendance for everyone. Russ and I considered providing a nurturing home environment as crucial as any other of our responsibilities.

We sometimes had memorable and funny experiences with our now larger-than-a-Brady-Brunch family. One nearly nine-year-old resident with a head full of cowlicks and a constantly dirty face seemed to have wanderlust. His empty seat at dinner usually signaled that he was off exploring. At times we found him on the tallest branch of the large oak tree next to our front porch, under the house surveying the pier and beam foundation, or on the fire-escape stairs looking for bird nests. When asked why he continued to find himself in destinations that got him in trouble, this little boy always replied, "'Cause I've never been there before." It was impossible to argue with this reasoning!

One year, we welcomed a sullen sixteen-year-old who wore all black. He was a loner who could be curt with Russ or me or anyone in authority. He complained that church wasn't his thing and made Sunday mornings difficult. We were surprised when an older couple from our church, who were aware of this resident's attitude, sought to be his sponsors. This meant they could take him out of the foster home on short visits. The resident protested that he didn't want sponsors of any kind, especially not "old ones." Then he surprised everyone when he started accepting their invitations to go home with them for dinner and dominoes. It was amazing to watch a real friendship develop between this patient hymn-loving elderly couple and our hard-rocker wanna-be. The resident sat with the couple in church sometimes and even called to check on them if they missed church. We discovered later that this resident maintained his friendship with the older couple even after he was released from our care and had moved away.

Positive experiences encouraged us and made us

aware that we were making a difference in our residents' lives. Unfortunately, we also had our fair share of runaways that kept us awake at night and on our knees praying for their safe return. There were years we were at the middle school and high school so often for conferences and disciplinary discussions concerning our residents that other parents assumed we were school staff. We were surprised on a regular basis by how much on-going training and social-worker intervention it took to meet the needs of some of our residents.

When periods of burn-out hit us, we'd wonder if what we did mattered. It would be just during this time we'd get to witness the reunification of a resident with his/her family. Or we'd receive a resident's much improved report card. We might also hear from a neighbor about some act of kindness by one of our residents. It would be just enough to encourage us to stay on another year.

We had remarkable successes and colossal failures in our eight-year tenure at the foster home. With God's help we learned big life lessons as a result of Russ's and my defining moment of signing those employee forms in 1981. We discovered that our efforts at providing the best home environment and using the most up-to-date guidance and counseling techniques were ineffective without God's leadership and help. "Whatever you do, work at it with all your heart, as working for the Lord, not for human masters, since you know that you will receive an inheritance from the Lord as a reward. It is the Lord Christ you are serving" (Colossians 3:23–24 NIV).

Those verses also validated another lesson we learned. If we put the Lord first and served Him, He would provide for us, even multiplying our meager salaries so that we thrived financially during those eight years.

Our foster-home years impacted the career paths of every member of our family. When we left, Russ decided to not go back to the business world. Instead, he used both his business background and the skills he had honed at the foster home to work in ministry. Until he retired in 2010, Russ worked with large churches in administration and as facilities director. Through the years our older daughter worked for three different Christian family-services agencies including the same one for whom Russ and I had worked. Our youngest daughter has served nearly twenty-five years as an ordained youth minister.

For myself, foster care helped me recognize the need for intervening and helping parents and children as early as possible. That led to my career in early-child development directing Christian-based childcare centers, helping to create and launch a parent mentoring ministry, and writing parenting and early-child-development curriculum.

A final lesson we learned came from our young resident with wanderlust: don't ever miss an opportunity to serve the Lord in a new, different, or challenging destination just because you've never been there before!

Dr. Dale E. Klein

DR. DALE E. Klein rejoined the University of Texas system in January of 2011 as associate vice chancellor for research in the Office of Academic Affairs. In April of 2010, after serving eight and a half years as a presidential appointee, Dr. Klein returned to Texas from Washington, DC, working at the University of Texas at Austin as the associate director of the Energy Institute, associate vice president for research, and a professor of mechanical engineering (Nuclear Program).

Dr. Klein was sworn into the US Nuclear Regulatory Commission in 2006 and was appointed chairman by President George W. Bush, serving in that role from July 2006 to May 2009. As chairman, Dr. Klein was the principal executive officer and official spokesman for the

NRC, responsible for conducting the administrative, organizational, long-range planning, budgetary, and certain personnel functions of the agency. Additionally, he had the ultimate authority for all NRC functions pertaining to an emergency involving an NRC licensee. The remainder of this term was as commissioner of the NRC from May 2009 to March 2010.

Before joining the NRC, Dr. Klein served as the assistant to the secretary of defense for Nuclear, Chemical and Biological Defense Programs. He was appointed to this position by President George W. Bush and confirmed by the Senate in 2001. In this position, he served as the principal staff assistant and advisor to the secretary of defense, deputy secretary of defense, and the under secretary of defense for Acquisition, Technology and Logistics for all policy and planning matters related to nuclear weapons and Nuclear, Chemical and Biological Defense Programs.

Previously, Dr. Klein served as the vice-chancellor for Special Engineering Programs at the University of Texas System and as a professor in the Department of Mechanical Engineering (Nuclear Program) at the University of Texas at Austin. During his tenure at the university, Dr. Klein was director of the Nuclear Engineering Teaching Laboratory, deputy director of the Center for Energy Studies, and associate dean for research and administration in the College of Engineering.

Honors and awards Dr. Klein has received include the Henry DeWolf Smyth Nuclear Statesman award in 2011, Fellow of the American Society of Mechanical

Engineers and the American Nuclear Society, Engineer of the Year for the State of Texas, the University of Missouri Faculty-Alumni Award, and the University of Missouri Honor Award for Distinguished Service in Engineering.

A native of Missouri, Dr. Klein holds a doctorate in nuclear engineering from the University of Missouri-Columbia. He has published more than one hundred technical papers and reports, and co-edited one book. He has made more than four hundred presentations on energy and has written numerous technical editorials on energy issues that have been published in major newspapers throughout the United States.

In addition to his academic assignments, Dr. Klein serves on the board of the Southern Company and the board of Pinnacle West/Arizona Public Service Company. He also serves on the Committee for Nuclear Power in the United Arab Emirates and chairs the Nuclear Reform Monitoring Committee for the Tokyo Electric Power Company following the Fukushima Daiichi nuclear accident.

Recalibration—Mission Trip to Guatemala

WE OFTEN GET involved in our work routines and do not think about how blessed we are living in the US. Our religious freedoms, travel freedoms, and freedom of expression are easy to take for granted. The cost and availability of travel, going to a pharmacy or to the grocery store, or the cost and availability of electricity are activities that are readily accessible to most US residents.

Simple tasks that we take for granted are not simple in many parts of the world. That is very apparent in rural areas of Guatemala. One example in rural Guatemala is buying medicine for a simple headache. First, it is likely that a trip to the drugstore would involve walking several miles. Calling for an Uber is not an option if you do not have a phone or the money for transportation. In fact, most people simply walk from one destination to another due to a lack of personal vehicles or even money for a bus, even if public transportation were available. Even if it were possible to reach a drugstore, there is still the problem of having the money to buy the medicine. Most of us in the US would not have great difficulty in paying a few dollars for a small bottle of Advil. This is not the case in rural Guatemala where many people are just concerned about their next meal.

We were blessed on these mission trips to Guatemala to work with a girls' orphanage. It was really more like a girls' home since several of the girls had been removed from their homes due to unbelievably abusive situations. Listening to some of the girls' abusive situations was shocking. Amazingly, many of these girls had adjusted to their new home in a very positive manner and for the most part had made remarkably positive changes in their lives. The specific home we were fortunate to impact was run by the Capuchin nuns. Religion played an important role in the lives of the girls in this home.

Unfortunately, the girls in the home and in other state-run programs had to leave the facility when they reached the age of eighteen. While the girls' home in which we worked did a great job of providing a safe and nurturing environment, they did not have the funding nor the infrastructure to provide the girls with a sustainable transition to living independently. Many of these girls faced an uncertain future when they had to leave at age eighteen.

On a very positive note, most of the girls were happy and had made an affirmative transition, spiritually and mentally, from an abusive situation to a safe and supportive environment. Many of these girls would tell our team that they did not just want our financial support, but mostly they wanted our love and our time. As you might expect, leaving these girls after having spent several days with them was very emotional.

Upon returning to the US, it was impossible not to thank God for our blessings and opportunities. Simple tasks like a cell phone call or getting into a car and going to run an errand had a new perspective. Most especially, previous priorities lack significance when you have the opportunity to change a life by donating seven days of love, time, and attention to children who are starved for it. I will always remember the blessings I am accorded and the ability to bless others profoundly with simply a smile, a warm embrace, and a listening ear.

Getting *Right* with God

IN THE SEVENTIES and eighties, state universities in Texas were under pressure to reduce prayers at public events. Part of this was driven by the fact that Madalyn Murray O'Hair's atheist organization was based in Austin, Texas.

I observed that several graduation programs gradually changed. Public events that started with a prayer were quietly modified to remove specific mention of Jesus. Initially, a reference to God was okay, but over time even this was discouraged and eventually eliminated.

I was fortunate to join the work at the Pentagon shortly after the attacks of 9/11/2001. Needless to say, I was pleasantly surprised that prayers were allowed and encouraged in the Pentagon. It was not forced on anyone, but it was welcomed. Many individuals commented on the fact that our founding fathers were strong supporters of freedom of religion. This did not imply that our founding principles were freedom *from* religion. There were many Bible study groups active during the lunch time throughout the Pentagon. On those occasions I had the privilege to have dinner at the home of a four-star general, it was always started with a prayer.

Upon reflection, it became clear to me why the military supported those that desired to pray privately and publicly. In the military, geopolitics can change quickly, and deployments to areas of conflict around the world can put one's life at risk. When your life is on the line, it causes individuals to evaluate their actions in a different perspective.

I was impressed by the number of service men and women who risked their lives for the benefit of others. The motto of "service before self" was demonstrated by both enlisted and officers repeatedly. I observed people many times making decisions that were based on what is right versus what is easy. These decisions were not made lightly and were not made for personal gain. In fact, many times decisions were made knowing that personal sacrifices might occur.

I was very impressed by the professionalism and the values of the men and women in uniform. They understood their mission and that sometimes this mission put them and others in harm's way. It seemed to me that many service men and women understood these risks and wanted to get their lives right with God in case they or their colleagues lost their lives.

These conversations with God started early and often with many men and women in uniform with whom I had the pleasure to serve. They knew the most important truth: waiting until the battle is not the first time to have a conversation with God.

Rebecca A. Klein

Rebecca A. Klein is principal of Klein Energy, LLC, an energy and water consulting company based in Austin, Texas. Her clients include international and domestic companies focused on penetrating or expanding in North America and whose needs concern regulatory, commercial, financial, strategic, and/or government affairs expertise. Over the last thirty years she has worked in Washington, DC, and in Texas in the energy, water, and national security arenas.

Ms. Klein served as chairman of the Public Utility Commission of Texas and ex-officio board member of ERCOT, during which time she oversaw the restructuring of the state's $36 billion electric power industry. She was also the chairman and vice chairman of the board of the Lower Colorado River Authority.

She has worked at the White House in the Office of Presidential Personnel where she assisted in recruiting and recommending sub-cabinet-level presidential appointees in the national security arena of government. Her experience in Washington, DC, also includes senior positions at the US Trade development Agency, the American Enterprise Institute, and as a senior fellow at Georgetown University's McDonough School of Business.

Ms. Klein serves on numerous boards, both privately held and publicly traded. Presently, Ms. Klein sits on the board of directors of both Avista Corporation and San Jose Water Group, a gas and power utility and a water utility respectively. Other boards on which she currently sits include two fast-growth technology companies serving the water and power industries. She is also the founder of the Texas Energy Poverty Research Institute, a nonprofit that addresses the nexus of energy and poverty in Texas. She has previously served on the Diversity Advisory Committee of the Federal Communications Commission. She has been recognized as Most Influential Corporate Board Director by *WomenInc.* magazine.

Ms. Klein retired as lieutenant colonel in the US Air Force Reserve in January 2015. She received her academic training at Stanford University (BA, Biology), MIT (MBA), Georgetown University (MA, National Security Studies), and St. Mary's Law School (JD). She is fluent in Spanish, having grown up partly in Venezuela and Mexico. She is a native of San Antonio, TX.

Mimo

Sometimes there are external events that happen to you that, like a pool ball, change your trajectory in life. And sometimes there are people who change not your trajectory but your entire approach to living. Because of them, over time, you're playing an entirely different game with different objectives and a new set of rules. That's what my grandmother did for my life. Without her, I would have been zipping forever across the same felt surface, pinging off the same four side walls, and plunging into the same six holes.

Blanca Cruz-Aedo Clark, affectionately dubbed Mimo, was seventy-six when she moved in with my parents and me in Austin, TX. I was eleven years old when Mimo came permanently into my life. My older siblings were no longer around, having married and starting their own lives. And so began my journey with my grandmother who, over the years, became my necessary caretaker, my undesired custodian, and ultimately my best friend.

My economics professor at Massachusetts Institute of Technology business school had a principle he called TATTOO—Thinking About The Thinking of Others. TATTOO is a game theory to gain strategic advantage over others in complex and interactive environments. To consider systematically how others may think about events, people, places, options, and situations is such a simple concept that we often overlook it. Well, utilized a priori, TATTOO can open new horizons. And when I apply TATTOO retroactively and consider in hindsight how Mimo must have thought of me, my parents, and her situation upon moving to Austin, I then understand the grand play she made in my life.

Mimo taught me five things that changed the way I view the world and how I strive to live each day.

Number 1: Be willing to face change at *any* stage in life. Mimo migrated from taking care of her own household to being a live-in caretaker in someone else's household. She left the city she knew and loved for most of her life to move to a strange town she had rarely visited. And that wasn't her final geographical change. Before she died, Mimo moved to three more cities with my parents. In conforming willingly to change, Mimo is a testament to what God says: "Do not be afraid or discouraged. For the LORD your God is with you wherever you go" (Joshua 1:9 NLT).

Number 2: Be flexible. For the last twenty-five years of her life, Mimo had to take on different roles. For a time she was my caretaker. Since both my parents worked, Mimo was there to greet me after school every day. She made dinner for us all, cleaned the kitchen, and babysat me whenever necessary. In my teen years, she was my guardian (although mostly she felt like my custodian). And in my adulthood, she became my confidant and best friend. Like a chameleon, Mimo met my needs at every stage of my life. She never held me to my past but encouraged me in every present moment. She understood that "For everything there is a season, a time for every activity under heaven" (Ecclesiastes 3:1 NLT).

Number 3: To give is to receive. Mimo spent her time mostly doing things for other people. She would crochet and sew incessantly. She made afghans and doilies for births and weddings and stitched blankets for holiday gifts. Mimo's blankets were particularly sought after. They are regarded by all as precious commodities. All our immediate and extended family members have some type of item hand made by Mimo. I believe this gave Mimo purpose. And when she presented any of us with one of her handmade treasures, she found joy in the appreciation and regard we held (and still hold) for her loving work. "Give, and you will receive. Your gift will return to you in full—pressed down, shaken together to make room for more, running over, and poured into your lap. The amount you give will determine the amount you get back" (Luke 6:38 NLT). I doubt Mimo memorized this verse. Then again, she didn't have to. She lived it.

Number 4: Controlling your mindset is pivotal to a happy day. Not every day was shiny and bright. There were times when Mimo got depressed. She would long for a call from one of her sons. Then there was the time another son lost his battle to pancreatic cancer. And sometimes, she would just wake up in the morning feeling sad and gloomy. One thing is certain, when the darkness of depression grips one person, the whole family is affected. My mother would remind Mimo periodically, "You can decide to be sad, or you can decide to be happy. No one can do it for you. It's ultimately up to you." Watching Mimo go through those cloudy days has caused me to realize that you can't dwell in the past or constantly plan and anticipate the future. What's important is the present moment and being grateful for all things and every person God has placed in my path. And that's how I've learned to "Be thankful in all circumstances, for this is God's will for you who belong to Jesus Christ" (1 Thessalonians 5:18 NLT).

Number 5: Changeless, unwavering love does not die. For the forty-one years I knew Mimo, her love for me never ebbed. It was constant, and she demonstrated it eagerly and persistently. No matter how much I annoyed her, hurt her feelings, or ignored her, she was always waiting to speak truth to me in love. In trying and sad times, she never lost faith in me. Over time, that gave me confidence in myself, a healthy self-awareness, and an aptitude to extend the love she first showed me. Mimo lived 102 years with a wonderful quality of life that awed even her gerontologist. Although she passed away twenty years ago, the consistent love she gave me and her family is everlasting. It continues to spread through each of us as we extend the love we first received from her to everyone around us. I am blessed to have her be such a true reflection of the fact that "the love of the LORD remains forever with those who fear him. His salvation extends to the children's children of those who are faithful to his covenant" (Psalm 103:17–18 NLT).

Freedom

THROUGHOUT HISTORY, CIVILIZATIONS have faced the tragedy of slavery and tyranny. We learn this in history books and spiritual books. As it is plainly stated in the Bible, "History merely repeats itself. It has all been done before. Nothing under the sun is truly new" (Ecclesiastes 1:9 NLT). The war in Ukraine today is no different than the scores of examples across millennia where the egoistic desires of one man are pitted against an entire tribe of people. The essence of each of these historical struggles centers around the principle of freedom.

As Americans, we often take for granted the freedoms we enjoy daily: freedom of choice, freedom of speech, freedom of religion, among many other ways we can each exercise our autonomy and independence. We forget the many people across the world that live under authoritarian foes and suffer economic and physical insecurity as well as violent conflict. It is because of sacrifice and battles, both physical and spiritual, that some societies can experience the gift of freedom today.

My appreciation for freedom was awakened in 1991 and has yet to be repressed. I was a young White House staffer and air force reservist. I was starting another busy day in my corner office of the West Wing of the White

House when my air evacuation squadron called me to announce I had four days to get ready to deploy to the Middle East. Saddam Hussein had just invaded Kuwait, and the world was coalescing to help the Kuwaitis regain their nation's sovereignty and freedom.

It was difficult to respond to my boss who asked why I was so quick to leave my prestigious post in the highest office of the land to travel to corners of the world that I never knew existed. How does one explain the need not to only fulfill an oath but also to avenge evil dictatorship and tyranny? Paul the apostle said it clearly: "For you have been called to live in freedom…use your freedom to serve one another in love" (Galatians 5:13 NLT).

As I disembarked from the huge C-5 transport plane, my senses became alert to my new surroundings. The land was flat and expansive. The air was dry, the sky was low, and the scent of sand filled my nostrils. As the night turned to day, I quickly absorbed what would be my new home and living conditions.

The weeks flew by as we worked long hours every day. Thanksgiving was punctuated with a big splash of excitement. The incessant chatter centered on whether the president would visit our location. Dare he come? Many doubted. When his trip was finally confirmed, I knew then how blessed we were having a national leader who took seriously the importance of fighting for freedom from sin and darkness.

The new year found us at a new forward undisclosed location. By this time the deadline the president set for Saddam Hussein to retreat was fast approaching. War was imminent, and tensions were high. Yet our morale was unwavering as we rushed to set up our new quarters, to build our new bunkers, to position the outhouses, and at the same time maintain our level of operability. We continued working twelve-hour shifts, seven days a week, and hardly noticed anymore the constant drone of low-flying jets overhead.

At 3:00 a.m. on January 17, we were bolted out of bed by the loud and piercing ring of the Scud alert siren. This time we knew things were different. The thunderous roars of the F-15, F-16, and A-6 jets, now laden with weapons under their wings, filled the sky as they took off in series heading to Baghdad. The liberation of Kuwait had begun. We had nine seconds to don our chemical masks and few precious minutes to jump into our chemical suits. We helped each other as we fumbled with the laces, the clasps, and the snaps. We then hastened to our sand bunkers outside, no longer recognizing the faces underneath the strange-looking masks.

Ninety long minutes passed when we fell into a hushed silence. We crouched low to the ground and strained to hear the voice over my short-wave radio. It was the familiar voice of our commander-in-chief. We clung to his every word, and I wondered whether my bunker mates could envision our president as clearly as I, having walked the same hallways with him in the White House. His words, full of conviction, reaffirmed my pride in being an American and a member of our armed forces. I felt that nowhere would I have rather been at that moment than crouched deep in a bunker with these new friends with whom I had trained, perspired, laughed, and cried.

When I returned home from conflict, I realized that my obligation to freedom was as important at home as on the battle front. I felt I had a responsibility to ensure that I was not oppressing those around me—family, friends, colleagues—by condemning them through my judgements, misplaced expectations, and faulty assumptions. I realized that each time I harbored such thoughts at home, work, or play, I was accusing, sentencing, and denouncing my brother. I was acting no different than a political despot, but merely in a different context. I was holding my brother in Christ in chains to my self-interests and desires. Yet when I have been set free from sin, I thereby set my fellow man free…from mental and spiritual oppression. And in turn, we are both slaves only to righteousness.

Today, when I read the newspaper headlines about the Ukraine-Russia conflict, I remember what it felt like to have a deep desire to give your life for your country and for peace and justice. My neck hairs rise reading about the men and women in Ukraine who are unrelenting in their quest for freedom and democracy. The Ukrainian spirit is a testament to us all of Jesus Christ's pronouncement that "There is no greater love than to lay down one's life for one's friends" (John 15:13 NLT). I pray for every Ukrainian who fights daily to preserve their homeland from the darkness of oppression.

Dr. Adena Williams Loston

Dr. Adena Williams Loston has served as the fourteenth president of St. Philip's College, one of our nation's Historically Black Colleges and Hispanic Serving Institution, since 2007. In January she was named one of the Ten Most Dominant HBCU Leaders of 2021. She possesses more than forty years of professional experience in both public and private sectors. Before coming to St. Philip's, she served as the chief education officer for the National Aeronautics Space Administration responsible for directing policy for $1.3 billion.

Her strategic leadership accomplishments include leading St. Philip's College to receive the 2018 Governor's Award for Performance Excellence, the 2018 national Malcolm Baldrige Award as one of the Alamo Colleges, and the 2020 Texas Award-Next for Performance Excellence. She has instituted Planning Budget and Assessment Cycles, Resource Allocation Processes, President's Academy, Department Chair Academy, Good to Great Strategic Planning Process, established three Centers of Excellence, and provided oversight for $400 million in new and renovated facilities construction.

For almost forty years, she was either the first or only African-American to serve in her capacity as she advanced in her career. Dr. Loston serves on many national, state, and local committees. Her academic preparation includes a bachelor of science degree from Alcorn State University (1973) and master of education and doctor of philosophy degrees from Bowling Green State University (1974/1979). She is the author of *The Ark of My Leadership Experiences*.

Overlooked

I was highly disappointed in being overlooked for the position that I thought was designed and perfect for me. I once worked in that particular higher education environment for ten years. The perfect opportunity opened up for me to return to that environment as a campus CEO. In my career journey I received elevated positions for the next fourteen years—associate professor, dean, and college president. Ultimately, I accepted a position in Washington, DC, as the chief education officer for the National Aeronautics and Space Administration. This was a high-profile position that I enjoyed greatly; however, after five years I decided that I want to return to higher education.

There was a position open at my former institution where I had dedicated ten years of service. It seemed like the perfect opportunity for me to return to my former institution, return to my family, return to my home, a familiar setup that was already in position. It all seemed ideal. I applied, interviewed, completed the open forums, completed a second round of interviews, successfully passed all reference checks, and the chancellor placed my name on the board of trustees agenda for appointment as president. It all seemed that I was about to return home.

However, it was not to be. That night at the board of trustees meeting, the board took no action on that agenda item. I was devastated because my opportunity to return home was squashed.

I reached out to my pastor to deal with my devastation. He decided to do some investigation to try and determine what happened. After consulting with one of the board of trustees members, I learned that months earlier, the board has advised the chancellor to cease and desist from making any major decisions. The selection of a college president in my mind is definitely a major decision. However, the chancellor ignored this advice and ignored the guidance from his board of trustees and continued the search process. My plans to return home, return to my family, sleep in my own bed, were crushed. The night that the board was to vote on my appointment was the same night that the board was buying out the chancellor's contract to send him on his way.

While I had prayed and asked my Father to close the door that I was not supposed to walk through, surely this was not what my Father intended. This could not be correct; however, it was exactly what my Father intended. He had another assignment for me. "Being still" was the message. I heard God saying, "'For I know the plans I have for you,' declares the LORD, 'plans to prosper you and not to harm you, plans to give you hope and a future'" (Jeremiah 29:11 NIV).

God needed me most in San Antonio at my current location where He has provided the increase, expanded growth, and enhanced programming. My defining moment was accepting that my Father actually did answer my prayers, just not in the way that I expected. He answered in a way that protected me in returning where I didn't belong; I had already satisfied my requirements in Houston.

Now, as I reflect on the outcome, I must admit that I spent too much time in despair, disappointment, and questioning. I had initially said it was the people that were involved that were blocking me from my blessings. Now, years later, it is so clear that we are not to design God's response nor His plans for our lives. His view and plans are far above our thoughts and ways. "Hope in the LORD and keep his way. He will exalt you to inherit the land" (Psalm 37:34 NIV).

Decision Point

UPON ARRIVING IN my new appointment, I quickly realized that in my new role as president of the college, twenty-five people reported directly to the president. Apparently, my predecessors saw this as a status symbol to have many individuals reporting directly to her; and of course, for the individual, that truly was an elevated status to report directly to the president.

For me this was an untenable situation. There was no time to think, process information, strategically plan, or engage in visioning for the future. My day was spent putting out fires or visiting with the individuals who reported directly to me and wanted access to their boss. Being the boss that I would like to have, I had an open-door approach, being readily available for individuals who reported to me. Constantly throughout the day, there was a knock at the door asking if we could talk. Or, the most popular question: "You got a minute?" The minute became five minutes, then ten, and then fifteen or up to thirty.

Ultimately, I had to make a decision. I could drown in reactionary approaches for twenty-five people, or I could restructure with a streamlined reporting structure—much like Jethro advising Moses while in the wilderness.

Jethro, Moses' father-in-law, arrived on the scene and observed Moses attempting to adjudicate the many issues that abounded in leading the masses to the Promised Land. It was impossible. He needed lieutenants. I needed a core team with fewer direct reports. For certain, less than twenty-five.

My span of control was too great, and my effectiveness was difficult to measure in overall efficiency. I was not dedicating valuable time to defining strategic objectives that would define and catapult the college into our future. No leader can be effective if her valuable time is solely dedicated to the immediacy of the day. Not only did I have to reference Moses, but I also had to reference Gideon. Gideon was going into battle with 32,000 volunteers, and when put to the test 32,000 became 10,000 and ultimately the victory was won with 300 folks.

Selection of the team that will take you to victory is ever so critical. It is with deliberate intention that the team must be tested either through you or by divine intervention. I also had to realize that everyone cannot go to the next level. By the time I had reached year five in my administration, the entire team save two individuals had changed. The core team consisted of three vice presidents, six deans, and two administrative support individuals for a grand total of twelve. Most important, only the three vice presidents and two administrative assistants reported directly to me. The decision allowed me to direct my attention, focus the leadership team, and take command of my day. This decision point allowed for a new focus, a new visioning with a new agenda for moving the institution forward.

"Commit your actions to the LORD, and your plans will succeed" (Proverbs 16:3 NLT).

Dr. Nora O. Lozano

NORA O. LOZANO, Mexican born, is executive director and cofounder of the Christian Latina Leadership Institute and teaches at the Doctor of Ministry Program at Central Seminary in Shawnee, Kansas.

She received her PhD and MPhil in religious and theological studies at Drew University, Madison, NJ; her MDiv at Eastern Baptist Theological Seminary, now Palmer Theological Seminary, Philadelphia, PA; and her BA in social communications at the Universidad Regiomontana in Monterrey, Mexico. In addition, she holds a doctor of divinity *honoris causa* from the John Leland Center for Theological Studies in Arlington, Virginia.

The work of the Christian Latina Leadership Institute is devoted to the discovery, development, nurturance, and empowerment of women leaders from a Latina perspective to be transformational agents in church and community settings.

Dr. Lozano has been involved in Christian theological education for more than twenty-five years. Her academic interests are centered in the areas of systematic, Hispanic, Latin American, and women's theologies as well as leadership studies. Her writings include chapters in books, essays in theological dictionaries and encyclopedias, devotionals, and Bible studies. In addition, she writes for digital publications such as *Baptist News Global, Baptist Standard, Good Faith Media,* and *Christianity Today.*

She is a member of the Baptist World Alliance Commission on Doctrine and Christian Unity and attends Woodland Baptist Church in San Antonio, TX, where she lives with her family.

New Beginnings

When I was five years old, I was attending kindergarten back in my hometown of Monterrey, Mexico. Ms. Beatriz—I remember her perfectly—was a great teacher, caring and encouraging. One day, she noticed that somehow we, the students, were wasting too much paper in our notebooks. So, on a particular Friday, she said: "Your homework is to fill a whole page following this pattern." I do not recall the pattern, if it was letters, numbers, squares, or circles. What I do remember is that she said that we could not waste paper in our notebooks, and that she would check on Monday if we had wasted sheets while completing this homework.

The next morning, I started to work on the homework, completely determined that I would not waste a sheet of paper. Well, guess what? I made a mistake! The more that I tried to fix my mistake, the more that a black spot began to spread on the page. Full of despair, I locked myself in the bathroom with my notebook and my sense of failure. Ms. Beatriz had said that we could not waste paper, and she would find out that I had wasted this sheet.

I am not sure how long I was there, until my siblings noticed that I would not come out from the bathroom.

They told my mother, and she came to see what was going on. After she knocked several times, ordering me to open the door, I finally opened it. I explained to her, with tears in my eyes, about my mistake, and what seemed like an insurmountable problem. She asked me to show her the page. She saw it for a minute, and then she forcefully tore the page out from the notebook. "There you go" she said, "start again."

I looked at the notebook. My mom had torn the page out in such a way that you could not even tell that it was there before. I could not believe it! Just like that, the sheet had disappeared! I began the homework again, and this second time I was able to do it just fine.

Of course, throughout my life, I have made many more mistakes, and I have returned again and again to this defining moment.

The Bible mentions that for those who are in Christ, they are a new creation: "Therefore, if anyone is in Christ, the new creation has come: The old has gone, the new is here!" (2 Corinthians 5:17 NIV). In the same way that my mother tore the page from my notebook, and opened a new opportunity for me, God offers us the possibility of new beginnings through Christ. This applies to all areas of our lives as well as to all of our relationships.

Often, I have wished that my mistakes could disappear as easily as the sheet of paper disappeared when I was five years old. Over the years, however, I have learned that often mending mistakes and starting anew requires intentional work.

First, we need to recognize and accept that we have done something wrong. Often this is hard work because we do not like to admit our mistakes. They may be too embarrassing or painful. However, the first step to start a change is to accept that something is wrong and needs to change.

Second, a new beginning normally requires some action on our side. On the one hand, it may be connected to the way that I relate to myself as I realize that I need to change a habit that is leading me on a path of destruction and death. On the other hand, it may be connected to the way that I relate to someone else. If this is the case, a new beginning may require apologizing to someone. If we want to have true and deep relationships, they need to be built on a strong foundation of honesty and responsibility. Recognizing that we have done wrong before God and/or a person may be hard, but it will set us on the path of new opportunities.

Third, a new beginning may also require accountability. Perhaps I need to look for a trusted friend or pastor who can keep me accountable so that I do not go back to my old behaviors.

Sometimes we are the ones who have made the mistake, and sometimes there are others who have treated us mistakenly. In the latter case, relationships may need a new beginning too. They may require new boundaries or limits as we develop a new way to relate to this person. At times, a new beginning may mean closing a relationship.

God has mysterious ways to offer us new beginnings.

Sometimes we may feel like that day that I locked myself in the bathroom thinking that I had this insurmountable problem. In the same way that my mother solved the problem in the most unexpected way, God may open different and unexpected paths.

As God opens new possibilities, it is normal that we may feel scared or hesitant to start anew. We must remember that we also have the constant intercession of Christ (see Hebrews 7:25), and the empowerment of the Holy Spirit (see Acts 1:8). Regardless of our failures or mistakes, the three members of the Holy Trinity are always luring us to new beginnings where we can experience divine grace, mercy, and a better future. Will we open the door?

A True Relationship

I GREW UP in a conservative, rigid religious environment where rules had to be followed and judgment and the possibility of punishment were always present.

Of course, the words *rigid, rules, judgment,* and *punishment* did not sound very appealing to me, or to anybody, I guess. On the contrary, they sounded harsh and scary.

Part of the rules, which came accompanied with judgement, was the practice of having a daily devotional that included spiritual disciplines. It was a must and the right thing to do. Period!

As many Christians, I also struggled with this daily devotional. And to be honest, I have to accept that I still do. Not in the same way that I did before, but still, it is a struggle.

What happened? How did things change?

The defining moment came when I grasped a deeper, and at the same time simpler, practical meaning of Christian spirituality. In his essay about spirituality in the *New Dictionary of Theology,* T. R. Alvin mentioned, "Christian spirituality involves the relationship between the whole person and a holy God, who reveals himself through both testaments—and supremely in the person of his unique son, Jesus Christ." As someone who has always thought theologically, I tended to gravitate to the most complex words in this definition. However, one day I just dwelled on the word *relationship*.

It is all about a relationship, I said to myself. It is not about rigid rules, judgement, and punishment, it is about a relationship! Once I discerned this, I started to put it in more practical ways as I pictured one of my important relationships.

I want to invite you to do the same. Picture an important relationship in your life: your spouse, children, grandchildren, or a good friend. If we really love them, we want to please them, we want to make them happy all the time. Let's think about a good friend.

Remember the day that you met one of your special friends. One day, you were introduced to this person, and you thought, *I really want to be friends*. So you started to try to find opportunities to spend time with this special person. And then the friendship started to develop and grow, and you invited your new friend to your house for dinner. And you asked, "Do you eat meat or are you vegetarian?" Because you wanted to serve a meal that would make your new friend feel happy and satisfied. And then you discovered the date of your new friend's birthday, and you tried really hard to find out what they might enjoy for a present, because you wanted to make them happy.

Now picture all this in your relationship with God. The Bible mentions that through Christ, we are made God's children (see Galatians 4:4–7). As such, we relate to

God out of love, not out of fear. In this relationship, we do the things that are going to bring glory to God. Or in simpler words, we do the things that are going to make God happy. In this relationship, we want to experience the joy of seeing our loved one happy.

How do we do that? In the same way that I want to spend time with this new friend and learn about what they like, Christians spend time with God through prayer, Bible reading, and meditation. These activities should not be seen as a burden but as a way to know more about this important person in our lives: God. They offer an opportunity to learn about what God likes and dislikes, as well as an opportunity to enjoy God's company.

Once I understood all this, the sense of obligation or fear of punishment regarding a daily devotional life disappeared.

Even with all this, as I mentioned earlier, I struggle with my devotional life, and I am sure that I am not the only one. Why do I struggle with this? This struggle is not related to a sense of fear but a sense of busyness. Life tends to get busy and complicated, and I struggle to find the time to invest in this important relationship.

What happens as a result of this? The consequences are not anymore related to guilt, punishment, or fear. When I am not intentional about my spiritual relationship with God, I am the one who is missing out. I am the one who is going through life without this special company. God is always there and ready to have a meaningful relationship with me, but I need to make the space for that.

Here is where the word *discipline* comes to the picture. Sometimes this word is associated with *punishment*. However, in Christian spirituality, *discipline* relates more to the constant practice of doing something. In this sense, discipline is something good that all human beings need. Discipline to eat well, to exercise, or to separate time to nurture our important relationships, including the relationship with God.

The moment that I discovered all this became a defining moment in my life. My prayer is that it will also become a defining moment in your life.

"Open your mouth and taste, open your eyes and see—how good God is. Blessed are you who run to him" (Psalm 34:8 MSG).

Norvi Maribel Mayfield

NORVI'S WORLDVIEW REFLECTS her humble beginnings as a Mayan Indian from the jungles of Honduras who is now an American citizen, a philanthropist, and a world traveler. With a degree from Honduras, she continued her education and theological studies at the Baptist University of the Americas and the Christian Latina Leadership Institute.

Called to missions since she became a Christian, Norvi was commissioned and licensed as a minister. Expanding her ministry, Norvi is the founder and executive director of Norvi Mayfield Ministries. She has been active in Christ-centered mission work in Mexico, India, Guatemala, Panama, Ecuador, Peru, Colombia, Honduras, Canada, Israel, and Iraq as well as empowering other mission entities serving in Africa and Asia. Norvi has been a volunteer translator for Open Doors, other Christian mission organizations, and churches.

Norvi is an engaging speaker for women's conferences, churches, Christian organizations, and humanitarian businesses/organizations. She trains short-term mission teams and serves as a consultant for Christian leaders here in the US and Latin American countries by assisting them in setting up nonprofit organizations and developing solid business models to sustain the ministry. She has been a strong supporter of the Christian Latina Leadership Institute and serves on the board of GRACE International.

Norvi and her husband live in South Texas. They have three adult children and two grandchildren. When not on the mission field, she is involved as a real-estate investor, ranch owner and manager, and as a Christian philanthropist.

Opportune Seasons for Heavenly Blessed Interruptions

THE DAY WAS beautiful and sunny, and I was lying in the fork of the branches of a mango tree nestled deep in a jungle mountainside of Honduras. It seemed the perfect spot to rest and enjoy some mangos after a morning of going up and down the mountain cutting and hauling pineapples. I can still taste the sweet mangos, like candy to me, and I still feel the soft jungle breezes blowing over me while I rested.

I was different and always so full of energy and curiosity that my father nicknamed me *Ocho con yo* Mayan girl. That was a derogatory idiom meaning "you little good-for-nothing Indian girl often sticking your nose in things where you shouldn't." For my father, seven was the perfect number, and I was number eight, *ocho*, meaning the leftover. It was on this morning that my life was interrupted as a couple passed by. They looked strange, and I thought they must be possessed to be out in the jungle as they were. I was soon to find out this *weird* couple lived not far from me on the jungle mountainside.

I say *weird* because they did not look like me or anyone I had ever seen. It was the first time in my life that I saw people who looked completely different than me. This *ocho con yo* Mayan girl followed them home. They lived in a simple home with a thatched roof, a dirt floor, and no running water. The doors and windows were basically holes that left them exposed to all the tropical jungle critters, including the venomous green snakes. I was so curious as to why golden-haired, blue-eyed persons would come to be with us.

I could hear them speak, and they did not speak like me, but somehow the sounds coming out of their mouth were like music to my ears. My curiosity made me spy on them all the more. They were forever tilting their heads and closing their eyes after reading a book they kept with them. Yes, you guessed it. They were reading their Bible and praying, and they were the first evangelical missionaries I encountered.

Years later, I realized that wherever a committed, faithful follower of Christ Jesus steps, claiming that ground for the Lord Jesus, then His presence is left there, and it becomes His holy ground where the Holy Spirit will move the souls. Yes, indeed, those times when they closed their eyes and tilted their heads, they were praying, and the prayers of the saints avail much. They planted the seed of salvation in me, but I did not know it at that moment. It took three years for those seeds to sprout. I became the only one in my family for many years who accepted Jesus Christ as my Savior.

I came to learn that these missionaries truly were possessed. I understood they were possessed with the Holy Spirit! Although I revered them, I still thought of them as *weird*. Well, the Bible calls them peculiar people. Years later, the Lord brought me to the United States to the little town of Gonzales, Texas, where I became the youth minister. I was blessed by the youth group with the name and title "Holy Weirdo." They thought I might shy away or scold them for giving me my new title, but what they saw was a response of great delight. I had graduated to be like the missionaries. I had become one weird, peculiar person for my Lord Jesus.

At this point of your reading, you are probably intrigued about why I entitled this story "Opportune Seasons for Heavenly Blessed Interruptions." "Opportune" because as I pass through God's prescribed days for my life on earth, His "heavenly blessed interruptions" have followed me through the seasons of my life and interrupted at God's chosen time. At times, I thought they were just interruptions, but I learned that they carry His blessings. They interrupted what I thought was my comfortable life.

But the day the golden-haired, blue-eyed, Bible-reading, praying missionaries interrupted my rest in the mango tree, my life took a different path. That moment set me for a complete 180-degree turn in my life. From that point, truly strange and unknown things began to come my way—things that I had no precedent for understanding or maneuvering through. It was God moving in my life, molding me more like Him, and giving me more opportunities.

I was a bare-footed Mayan Indian girl who knew only the jungle, how to make tortillas, and run up and down the mountain collecting wood to cook our next meal. I washed clothes on the rocks by the spring water while fighting mean monkeys that would gang up on me to take my clean clothes to the canopy of the five-to-ten-story-high ceiba trees.

Think of the blessed interruptions it took to bring me from the Honduran jungles to where I am today. God moved mightily to bring me to the United States, where I have learned to speak English and am learning Korean, Hebrew, and the Syriac Aramaic languages. I drive a vehicle, wear high heels to church, and I am a cattle and timber rancher. I am the daughter of the King, and I give witness wherever He gives opportunity.

Reflect over your life. Has God interrupted you and caused you to change paths? I'm certain if God had plans to bring a simple Mayan girl out of the jungle and give her opportunities for education, world travel, and speaking His truth to large and small groups, He has a plan for your life too. Blessed interruptions that brought me from light to darkness, from dictatorship to freedom. Only God! Only our mighty God can do that.

Me? I'm Personally the Answer to Someone's Prayer?

HAVE YOU EVER been told that you are personally the answer to someone else's prayer? It was one of the most humbling experiences in my life. Let me tell you about my moment.

It begins on a summer morning in South Texas where you would have found me deep among the pastures, mesquite, huisache trees, and cacti of my two-hundred-acre cattle ranch in South Texas. I was minding my own business that morning, milking my two jersey cows. Wearing my black rubber boots that came to my knees, I was walking back home from the cattle pins after milking and feeding the cows some protein grain cubes. I could feel the summer's heat through those boots as I carried two pails of rich, creamy jersey milk.

Of course, like a good Honduran girl who had become a Texas ranch woman, I carried my trusted machete. I grew up accustomed to the snakes in the jungle, and I knew the Texas countryside has some good-sized venomous snakes—rattlesnakes sunning around the cattle pens and the barn or the copperheads lurking around the area surrounding our house. I had learned to always be prepared even while carrying two large pails of milk.

Ms. Elizabeth Elliot's paraphrase of a Bible verse had become my motto: "Work hard with your hands and mind your own business." So, there I was working and minding my business that hot summer morning, and I did not know that God was already working, minding His business, and getting ready to tell me I was about to do His work in another part of the world.

When I got home, I started to fill the sterilized milk bottles with the fresh milk. Earlier, before I left for the barn, I had taken out some gallons of milk from the day before. The milk was waiting for me to turn it into mozzarella cheese, butter, and whey—ingredients I was planning to use to make the dough for the pizza for our evening family meal. I was working and minding my business when the phone on the wall rang. Those were the days when we only had landline phones. I was blessed to afford one. I cleaned my hands and answered it.

I was truly not expecting what I heard. It was a request for me to be a Spanish translator and a mission-trip leader. It had been a long time since I had been fully engaged on the mission field. During this season of my life, my work and my business were being a wife, mom to three children, helping my sister with her two daughters, and being a ranch hand. Then there were all the in-between chores like the continual work of building of our straw-bale house, cooking, making cheese, butter, aromatherapy soaps, and sewing. Yes, we lived in a solid and well-built straw-bale house. We were careful to build it correctly so that it would withstand the natural elements.

God's blessed knock on the door of my life that morning was quite a surprise. In the hustle and bustle of my daily activities, I was not anticipating such a great visitor. His knock was a heavenly, blessed interruption. The gentleman on the phone stated that the trip would be to the persecuted Christians in Chiapas, Mexico. This was at the time when persecution of Christians was at its worst in the area. Many men had been given a life sentence for spreading the Gospel of Jesus as pastors or church leaders. One of the main purposes of the trip was to encourage their wives, who were considered widows, their children, and to try to encourage the brethren held at a maximum-security prison. I could only say yes to this blessed interruption in my life.

Weeks later, I found myself in mountainous jungles like my homeland of Honduras—mountains covered in a lush, green rainforest—but this time, the jungle was in Chiapas, Mexico. We drove for hours from San Cristobal de las Casas out to the mountains. We parked the van and started our hike up the mountain range until we came to a clearing. In weeks prior to our arrival, our local contact pastor had sent messages through the mountains that we would be coming to all the widows. We had been praying for their safety as they would come to meet with us at this remote spot in the mountain range.

We waited and prayed for over two hours, and one by one the widows and their children started to show up. I had been pacing the red, muddy clay path cut from the side of the mountain, always looking down, waiting to see if more were coming. After three hours of being there, I caught a glimpse of a silhouette starting to appear from down the mountain. The silhouette of a tiny older lady came into focus as she walked faster and faster, her face like flint focused on me. As she drew nearer, I could see this beautiful, frail older woman, her Mayan outfit so worn and tattered. It takes years to make one complete Mayan outfit, and it is usually worn for life. Her patched huipil, skirt, rebozo, and headpiece revealed the patches and repairs done through the years.

Who knew how many hours she had been walking to get to this spot to meet us? She was breathless and looked like she had given it all just to make it up the mountain. She was one of my Mayan elderly grannies to whom I owe respect. According to my culture, I could not look her straight in her eyes until she had first addressed me and given me my blessing. And so she did. She came to within ten feet of me, her small eyes peeking through wrinkled eyelids focused on me—like she recognized me! Then she embraced me. She spoke to our translator in Tzotzil Mayan dialect. Even so near out of breath, she spoke excitedly, trying to get her words out. All along she had me in her embrace.

Have you ever been hugged by a saint that walks so close to the Lord that you feel so unworthy, so convicted of your own sins, that the only response is to fall to your knees? So that was me in those moments. I looked at the director of the trip and asked what I should do? I felt filthy and guilty and not worthy to help her. He told me to let go, give myself to her, and that God would do the rest.

I learned she was the matriarch of these region. So now not only the eyes and attention of the trip director were on us, but all the widows, children, and all the team members became our audience.

My sweet Mayan granny proceeded to tell our Tzotzil translator pastor, "Tell her that the Lord has given her to me in visions. I have seen her in my visions many, many moons ago. I have been praying to the Lord, asking if there no other Christ-believing people in these mountains. I prayed, 'Help us, Lord, for we have lost everything in our lives, truly everything.'"

Then the older woman added, "Tell her the Lord has sent her to me, to us. She is the answer to my prayers and visions. In my visions I saw her just like she is, and behind her there was a multitude of peoples. In my visions I could never touch her or the multitude of peoples, but today as I hold her in my arms, I have touched the peoples. All is fine! All is good! God has given His answer. She is here."

She paused throughout her conversation as she shed tears of thanksgiving. Then she spoke again to the translator. "Ask her how many days she walked to get to us?"

You must understand that Mayans measure distance by how long one walks. I looked at the director again, and he just looked back at me as if to say, "You have the answer." How could I explain to this precious saint that it only took a four-hour flight to Mexico City from San Antonio, Texas, and two hours to fly to Chiapas. But all that came to my mind was that a year has 365 days. So, I answered, "Three hundred and sixty-five days' walk was my trip."

Her tear-filled eyes looked at me with such gratefulness. Her heart was so full! I explained that many have been the saints and the churches that made my trip possible to come to see them. And I was carrying with me their love and support. And thus began my ministry to the widows of Chiapas.

Our Lord tells us, "Here I am! I stand at the door and knock. If anyone hears my voice and opens the door, I will come in" (Revelation 3:20 NIV). Our Lord will visit us throughout our days, but are we ready when He comes? He comes when we least expect Him, even on a summer morning after I milked the cows. I confess I was being a busy Martha, but when God surprised me with that invitation, I was ready to be Mary, to sit at His feet, and do His bidding. I would have missed one of the greatest and most humbling moments in my life if I had not accepted His invitation. That is the reason our Lord encourages us to be ready in season and out of season. "Preach the word; be prepared in season and out of season; correct, rebuke and encourage—with great patience and careful instruction" (2 Timothy 4:2 NIV).

In His wisdom, the Lord created you, gave you your parents, your nationality, your time in history, gender, life circumstances, and the uniqueness of you! For through your obedience to Him, you will be the living answer to prayer for someone that only you will be the right fit to fill their hearts.

I am grateful to my two spiritual mentors—Brother

Bill and Ms. Phyllis, as I call them—for encouraging me to write these two stories. So now I encourage you to write your stories, for in your written word, you will be imitating our God. He inspired and encouraged the Bible writers to write about who He is and the immense love He has for us all. Let us be in flesh and blood God's healing or encouraging ointment for someone who is crying out to heaven. Let us be holy weirdos for our Lord. Let us be His peculiar people. All these words and my life are to honor Him who chose me to be His. It is all about Him!

Merlin Merritt

MERLIN MERRITT WORKED in spaceflight operations at NASA's Johnson Space Center in Houston from the early Gemini program throughout much of the shuttle program. He was one of the lead engineers on Apollo 11 and during the Apollo 13 crisis that helped develop the procedures for the safe return of the crew.

During his work there, Merlin felt the call to pursue a theological career, and after twenty-eight years, he retired from NASA and became a minister of Christian education serving a church in Houston. He later became an adjunct professor of training foundations and biblical studies at the Baptist University of the Americas in San Antonio.

He and his wife, Shirley, have been part of numerous

short-term mission trips to several Central and South American countries sharing their story of faith. Merlin is now retired and speaks widely at various schools, universities, churches, and para-church organizations, sharing his message of faith and science. He has authored two books, *Seeing the Son on the Way to the Moon: A NASA Engineer's Reflections on Science and Faith* and *Merlin's Magic Mission Trip: An Adventure of Good vs. Evil in the Amazon Rainforest.*

Calling

I believe every person is called by God—young or old, male or female, white or black, without regard to ethnicity or race, we are all called by God. We know from Scripture that God is not willing that any should perish.

These callings are defining moments in our lives. Now there are different kinds of callings: there is the calling to our eternal salvation; there is a calling to some special service, or a special task; and a call to full-time vocational ministry such as a pastor or worship leader. These may come at different times in our lives, or they may be simultaneous. The apostles appear to be called to salvation and a full-time calling to be "fishers of men" at the same time. The apostle Paul, on the other hand, had a dramatic conversion experience on the road to Damascus, spent several years ministering to the church in Antioch, and later was called to go on a mission trip (actually, several).

These callings are like hinges or defining moments in our lives when we sense the movement of God in a special way, and our lives are forever changed. We may not hear a verbal call, but definitely a special sense of God's Spirit. It may be the miraculous working of external circumstances that fall into place, giving us direction or urging us to move in a certain direction. These are God moments, and we cherish them highly.

I have never heard God speak to me in an audible voice, but there have been times in my life when I felt His Spirit so real and so intense that I knew my spirit resonated with His Spirit, and that moment shaped my life. One such moment in my life occurred when I was a sophomore in college attending a Baptist student retreat. Although I had been baptized and accepted Christ as a twelve-year-old boy, my life as a youth had no real spiritual depth, and church for me was pretty much fun and games.

Upon high-school graduation I enrolled at the University of Texas at Arlington, which was not far from my home in Fort Worth. I enrolled as an electrical engineering student because I liked the study of electricity and had good grades in math and science. I had several friends at the school's Baptist Student Union (BSU), and I often made my way to the noon luncheons to get a free meal and meet girls.

In the spring of my sophomore year I was invited to a BSU retreat in the piney woods of East Texas. It was a picturesque setting and seemed like a nice weekend with games and fun activities. I had broken up with one girlfriend and was looking for someone new to meet.

On Saturday of the retreat, something happened that shaped the rest of my life. As we gathered for a meeting that Saturday morning, part of the program involved a visiting pastor bringing an inspirational message. He spoke on the story of Jesus talking with a Samaritan woman who had come to a well to draw water. If you're not familiar with the story, it's found in John 4, but basically it's the story of this woman who has drifted from living with five men and is looking for meaning and love in her life. Jesus bridges the gender, racial, and religious gaps of society and drives to the core of the woman's need, which was spiritual. After the woman's background is revealed by Jesus's supernatural insight, the woman tries to divert the conversation to question where people should worship. Jesus then declares to her that true worship is found in spirit and truth regardless of the location. Through that experience she came to realize He was the Messiah. She drops her water pot and runs into town to tell everyone.

The message spoke to my heart.

Now at the end of the pastor's message he asked us to do something a little different. He asked each of us to leave the room and go find a place outside to be alone with God and pray. Well, being somewhat adventurous, I wandered off from the meeting at least a mile or two into the woods. I followed this little trail through the woods, and then to my amazement I came to a small clearing with, of all things, an ancient-looking water well. What it was doing out there in a deserted part of the woods, I'll never know (God knows).

In the moments that followed, I experienced the presence of God like I never had before. The presence of the well coupled with pastor's message on the woman at the well resonated with my heart and soul. Although I had never lived with any girlfriends as the woman in the story had, I had bounced around from girlfriend to girlfriend, and I had no direction in my life. I dropped to my knees, confessed my sin, and committed to the Lord that I would follow Him in life wherever He would lead. I did not know where He would lead, but I just knew I wanted to serve Him.

I returned to the camp with a sense of joy and calling I had never experienced before. It was definitely an encounter with God and defining moment that set the tone for my entire life.

In the two years that followed, I was still a little undecided on which direction to take, but I sensed God was leading. I continued my engineering degree, and when it came time to graduate, I found myself sending out résumés to many of the large engineering corporations. As engineering students were in high demand, all my friends were getting several good offers, and although I had good grades, I only got one offer. That was from NASA. So, if I wanted to eat, I would have to pack up and move to Houston. The amazing thing, however, was that I secretly wanted to work for NASA. I had recently heard President Kennedy's "Go to the Moon" speech, and my soul resonated with that calling.

Also, I realized I could partner with my good friend who had just moved to Houston. We teamed together as a music and comedy act and volunteered with an organization called Youth for Christ. It was a great avenue for Christian witness, as we not only shared our testimonies at numerous churches but also were allowed to enter high schools and share our act and testimony there. We even once performed at the Houston Music Hall as part of the Youth for Christ program.

As I mentioned in the opening paragraph of this story, I believe we are all called by God. These moments may not be as dramatic as Paul's call on the road to Damascus, or even finding a water well in the middle of nowhere, but I believe we are all brought face to face with God at some point. The water-well experience for me was certainly a defining moment in my life from which I was forever changed.

Apollo 13

THE STORY OF Apollo 13 has been told several times and even made into a feature film. Although the dramatic events of that mission happened over fifty years ago, that mission was a defining moment in my life. I was just a young engineer working at the Mission Control Center in Houston as part of the team that developed the procedures that led to a safe return of the Apollo 13 astronauts.

Several said the flight was a failure, but for me the flight of Apollo 13 was not a failure but a flight of miracles. What most of the books and movies don't tell you is this: there were actually several miracles God performed that allowed the crew to return safely to the earth. It was a flight protected by the Creator of life Himself who reached out to protect the crew and provide a lifeboat for three astronauts whose lives literally hung in the balance of space.

Apollo 13 lifted off on April 11, 1970, under the power of the giant Saturn rockets. It was our third flight to the moon and more ambitious than the first two. After earth orbit the flight plan of Apollo 13 had the Command and Service Module (CSM or mother ship) and the Lunar Module (LM or landing vehicle) separate from the booster and leave on a trajectory toward the moon. It was over 238,000 miles to the moon and took about three days. On April 13 the spaceship was over halfway to its destination, and I had just arrived on my shift in the control center when the now famous words floated ominously down through space, "Houston, we have a problem." Four rows of flight engineers watched intensely and huddled over the telemetry data from the spacecraft.

At first the data on the computer screens was scrambled, and we weren't sure if we were experiencing real problems or merely bad telemetry data. The voice of Jim Lovell was calm, so calm, that no one at that moment knew the extent of the disaster that had just occurred. Because sound waves do not travel in space, astronauts Lovell, Haise, and Swigert had not heard the violent explosion that had just ripped open the side of their spacecraft. Their first reaction had been to a bang like a thud accompanied by some vibrations.

Onboard, the red master alarm flashed, indicating a serious problem. At the control center, after obtaining solid data, we recognized we had lost an oxygen tank and the other tank was leaking. My fellow flight controllers also soon recognized that we had major power failure. The bad thing about losing oxygen was that it was not only our source of breathable atmosphere for the crew, but oxygen was also our primary source of power on the mother ship, the fuel-cell power system requiring oxygen to generate electrical power. With the reality of the loss of the oxygen system and loss of the primary power supply, we quickly realized that not only had the mission to the moon been lost, but we would soon be fighting just to keep the crew alive. The obvious immediate choice was to power up the Lunar Module just to provide a safe haven.

The Lunar Module was never designed to enter the earth's atmosphere, but it could be used as a lifeboat. I was the primary Lunar Module engineer on shift, and our first task was developing the appropriate procedures to power up and stabilize the LM. I believe God's hand was guiding us as this was not a simple task. After the LM was successfully powered up and the crew transferred, we spent the next suspenseful minutes calculating the available life support consumables—power, water, and oxygen.

We faced the seemingly impossible challenge of making the LM lifeboat, which was designed for two men for only one day, last for three men for three and a half days. As it turned out we had enough oxygen, but power and water, which were needed to cool and run the equipment, were projected to run out long before our earth entry. Our initial estimate of the consumable usage rate was so chilling some engineers thought we should turn the vehicle around immediately and perform a direct abort back to earth.

After considerable analysis and discussion, we reached a decision to use the Lunar Module engine instead of the CSM engine to send the entire spaceship in a slingshot maneuver around the moon back to earth and then power the systems down to conserve consumables. I believe God was guiding us as we made those choices, and all the systems worked appropriately. In fact, Gene Kranz, our flight director, later said, "Through some miracle, a burst of intuition, something we had seen or heard or felt told us, don't use the CSM main engine."

After the power down, the data still indicated it would be very close as to whether we would make it. However, again I believe it was God's miraculous power that reached out and stretched the life-support consumables to enable the LM, much like Jesus himself broke five loaves of bread and two fish some two thousand years ago to feed the five thousand.

At 9:00 a.m. the next morning, my shift was over. I'll never forget that day. As I went home the events of the tense hours revolved in my head. At home I turned on the TV, and there to my surprise was the CBS national anchor, Walter Cronkite, relaying our story to a waiting world. One of the amazing things that happened was the tremendous outpouring of prayer across the country and even worldwide. Special prayer vigils were called, and even the pope issued a proclamation that all people should pray. I, too, prayed for the three astronauts whose lives literally hung in space.

That evening, as my next shift began, our bleak projections seemed a little better, but we were still not out of the woods. We spent the next couple of days ensuring minimal power levels for the crew and spaceship. As the spaceship traveled back to earth, we continued to feel God's presence guiding us as the crew faced harsh conditions inside the spaceship, and other problems began to surface.

As we continued our perilous journey back to earth, several other incidents of life-threating circumstances challenged us. I believe God inspired and enabled us in the design and fashioning of a makeshift carbon-dioxide removal system. It was made from cardboard and duct tape, which averted the buildup of dangerous levels of carbon dioxide. The charging of our re-entry batteries could only be accomplished with the miraculous forethought of a charging wire that had been added to the ship years earlier for a separate reason.

Also, and perhaps most astonishing of all, the forecast of a hurricane developing over our intended landing site in the ocean miraculously dissipated and moved away Then, after three days of hazardous and extreme conditions, the crew landed safely in the Pacific Ocean on April 17, 1970. All of these incredible events, I believe, were overcome by an omnipotent God in response to prayer.

For me, Apollo 13 was a defining point in my life. A few years down the road, I felt God calling me to full-time vocational ministry in Christian education. I left NASA, attended seminary, and became a minister of education at a Baptist church in Houston. The Lord has used my story as a platform to speak at numerous churches and other organizations across the US and foreign countries, showing how God uses all things, and at times even catastrophic circumstances, to accomplish his purposes and work for good.

Andy Muck, MD

BORN AND RAISED on a dairy farm in western New York, Andy could stack hay with some of the best. He graduated with a bachelor of arts in molecular biology in 1999 at Colgate University, Hamilton, NY. He attended Johns Hopkins School of Medicine, earning his MD in 2004. Following medical school, he completed an emergency medicine residency with the military in San Antonio.

Andy joined the air force to see the world, and saw Texas, Iraq, and Afghanistan. After leaving the air force, he settled in the San Antonio area. He has worked in education for over a decade and helped start the emergency-medicine training program at the University of Texas Health at San Antonio, where he continues his work as professor/clinical in the Emergency Department and co-director of the San Antonio Refugee Health Clinic. He now works as an ED physician in the Christus Health System with Victoria Emergency Associates.

He has been married to his wife, Kelly, for twenty-two wonderful years. They have four children, Anna Beth (18), Will (16), Sadie (13), and Hayes (6). He farms in his free time and trains anyone interested in how to milk.

Set Free

IN 2010, I was deployed in support of Operation Enduring Freedom in Afghanistan. I was deployed as an emergency medicine physician as part of a Critical Care Air Transport Team (CCATT). I was leaving behind my wife, Kelly, and three young children. After a previous deployment to Iraq, I had learned the hardship of being away from your family to be somewhere that seems a million miles away from home in so many different ways.

As a CCATT physician, I was part of an amazing system of caring for critically injured service members in Afghanistan. I helped run a flying intensive-care unit with my outstanding team of a critical-care nurse and respiratory therapist. We could fly almost anyone anywhere, no matter how ill, to get them to the next-level hospital in Afghanistan, Germany, or the US.

After my previous deployment in Iraq, and now into this deployment, I had seen destruction that caused me to lose myself and some of my identity. I began to see a cruelty in the world. I had trouble reconciling my views on people, the world, and God. My relationships in my life were affected. My view of my own being had been infected with a darkness.

By this point in my career, I had seen death. However, there was something unique to me about the death I saw overseas in war. The deaths were so fresh. The death was so brutal, raw, and abrupt. I saw men who the day before were at the prime of their existence. Then dead, wrapped in a flag, and being flown back home. I saw their friends with the emptiness in their eyes that comes with a lost hope and wounds that don't heal.

As the deployment in Afghanistan was progressing, I felt the creeping of darkness deeper inside. Every flight we took and every patient I transported, I saw less reason, less hope, and a feeling of doors closing. We kept having things go wrong on our flights and back on base. The world seemed to be against us, and all seemed to be covered in a dark cloud. As if the world wanted to provide a physical manifestation, a volcano erupted in Iceland. This volcano was spreading a cloud of ash into the skies around Europe. We kept being able to fly CCAT missions into Germany, but we were unable to fly our teams back to Afghanistan. After a short time, several of our teams were stuck in Germany.

Finally, the volcano provided a break. A KC-135 plane, the air-refueling plane that we often used as a vehicle of opportunity to fly CCATT missions, was free to take several of our teams back to Afghanistan. The plane was loaded very heavily with multiple CCATT and air evacuation groups.

Our plane took off without anything unusual. We came to cruising altitude over the skies of Germany and were headed back to theater. As everyone settled in for a lengthy flight back to Afghanistan, everything went completely silent. I experienced weightlessness. I looked over at one of the respiratory therapists, and we both knew we were in free fall. We also knew we were going to die and there was nothing we could do about it. There was no screaming, there was no yelling. Only silence. There was simply a clear acceptance that this was the end.

After the hours that are only seconds in a near-death experience, the plane shuddered as the engines came back on for a brief moment. Again, the engines stalled, and we again fell. I thought of my kids. I thought of my wife. I thought of how different their lives were going to be. I thought about my own life, and thought to myself, *Really, this is how it ends?*

Then the plane shuddered, shook, and the engines restarted. The smell of smoke filled the cabin. We put on our oxygen hoods and waited for the engines to stall again. The engine didn't stall again. We returned to Germany and landed the plane.

Despite the shared physical experience, the emotions experienced in such moments can be very individual. In my dark view of the world, combined with this event, I was enveloped in a pitch darkness, a vacuum void of hope. Despite surviving, I fell into a pit of fear that was all consuming. The hopelessness I was experiencing had led to an impotence in performing my function as a critical-care physician and as a team member. I realized I had become absolutely convinced I wasn't going to make it home.

My wife is my lifeline to the world. Her thoughts and my conversations that I have with her are the lens through which I see the world. She helps me interpret and process the things I see around me. My life is so integrated with hers that when anything crazy happens, I just know one thing for certain—I need to speak to my wife as soon and as much as possible. I called my wife every chance I could get as I dealt with this near disaster.

I shared with my wife how I was scared. Every turbulent bump on a plane meant I was going to die. I was living with a void of light of which I could not get out of. I thought I was scared for my kids. I was perseverating on my kids growing up without a father and how this would destroy them.

In one single call to my wife, with one statement, it all changed. In one particular intense conversation when I was melting down, my wife stopped me. She said she needed me to know something. She said the following: "Our lives would be very hard if something happened to you, but we would be fine. I need you to know that we will be okay if you do not come home."

I broke into tears. I experienced a recognition of my frailty, my consuming fear, my selfishness, and my lack of faith. In that moment, I experienced freedom. So much of my fear came from a place of self-protection, not of love. I was actually much more worried about myself than I realized.

One would not think that your wife telling you that she'd be fine without you could be a defining positive moment. However, I am bathed in my wife's love and knew that it came from a place of compassion. In one statement, she set me free. She set me free from the consuming thought that I was responsible for everything that could happen to me and my family. She also put me in my place, reminding me that I am not God. I could never care for my family the way my Father in heaven could. I could never protect my family, my wife, nor my children. I only had one thing to do: to rest myself and my family in the loving hands of my Savior.

I have lived with a renewed sense of peace since that day. I pray with more purpose. I know my place in this world. I trust in my God that He knows the numbers of the days of myself and my family. I need not fear. I have little to do but to worship God and enjoy Him forever.

What It Means to Be Poor

I GREW UP on a dairy farm in western New York. This was a formative experience, as I still to this day know a thing or two about milking. I don't like to brag, but I can really milk a cow. People think knowing how to milk is not an important life skill, but I would argue that it insures I will never go without milk on my cereal or cream in my coffee.

I remember milking cows fairly regularly by age eight. I was too short to plug the suction and pulsator into the pipeline. I would have to crawl up the stanchion where the cow was tied to be able to attach the milking machine. I remember many very cold mornings and nights, with piercing wind, freezing rain coming down, or snow all around. I definitely had to walk uphill both ways as the wind would blow and there would be shifting snow drifts.

It was a challenging way to grow up. You can just ask my kids, as I tell them almost daily how hard I had it and how easy they have it. I have further educated my kids with my knowledge of milking. I have told them repeatedly that I may not be a great parent. I might not teach them all the important life skills. However, they will know the six dairy cow breeds and how to milk. I often tell them how lucky they are to have me as a father, telling them how good they have it now. I'm not sure they've got it yet, so I continue to provide them daily reminders of how spoiled they are and how they are very lucky. My kids are lucky because of all the modern conveniences, I tell them, but also lucky to have me as a father to constantly remind them how lucky they are.

I grew up in a Civil War-era farmhouse on a two-hundred-acre farm. Our house was full of history you could feel in every room. Some of the barns were very old. I had fantastic adventures playing in hay mows with my brothers, imagining what it must have been like to farm in this place without all the luxuries of tractors and equipment that we had. We had old tractors and some very old equipment, but it all got the job done as we planted and harvested each season.

My brothers and I worked hard for my father, particularly during the spring and summers. My dad paid us by the hour. It wasn't a lot, but I could always save my money up long enough to do what I wanted. I never asked my father for money because I knew I was getting paid. If I wanted more money, I would work and save.

I felt proud of my dad. We had barns and equipment. My father, unlike most of my friends' fathers, owned his own business. He managed one hundred milking cows, replacement heifers, and managed two hundred acres of crops. My family was generous with those around them, always being willing to lend a hand to those who needed it. From my vantage point, I felt like we were doing just fine. From the perspective of a kid, we had some stressful times with crop failures or a cow dying, but it all seemed to work out fine in the end.

When I was an older teenager, I helped my dad prepare the taxes. You could imagine with a small business and a farm, keeping track of all the expenses and incomes was challenging. The exercise of having me help prepare the taxes was eye opening on many levels. I saw where money was spent, how we gained our income, and how small prices in the change of milk had a big impact at the end of the year.

The biggest surprise in helping my father prepare taxes was to find out that our income was below the federal poverty level that year. I was shocked. I asked my dad what terrible thing happened this particular year that we had so little income. My dad then told me that this was similar to all the years he had ever farmed. We had never made any more money than we had that particular year.

I was absolutely astounded to find out I was poor (according to the government). I grew up feeling wealthy my entire life. My dad owned his own farm and didn't owe the bank a cent. We always had food on the table. I had loving parents who cared for me. I had a creek to enjoy, giant fields to run around, hills to sled on, a big house to enjoy, plenty of animals, and many pets. I had everything a kid could want. Here it took the government to help me find out I was actually living in poverty.

This was the moment I learned sometimes being poor is a state of mind. As long as you have some good food to eat, a place to live, and some wonderful family, a poor kid like me might never know he was poor. There is no question that true poverty and starvation exist. It is not a joking matter and affects many. However, it is also true that at times we look around and see the wealth of others and can fool ourselves into feeling like we are going without. We become too consumed with comparison and not paying attention to the blessings we have been given.

It was only later, when I had much more money, that I sometimes felt like I didn't have enough. Then I also learned, no matter how much I had, I had been fooled into always wanting a little bit more. As I learned to trust more in the Lord and the provisions He had given me, I could again remember the lessons I learned as a teenager. You can be rich in spirit without having much, feel wealthy because of the relationships with which you have been blessed, and rest in where the Lord has placed you.

In the Gospel of Matthew, we learn something about God's provisions:

> That is why I tell you not to worry about everyday life—whether you have enough food and drink, or enough clothes to wear. Isn't life more than food, and your body more than clothing? Look at the birds. They don't plant or harvest or store food in barns, for your heavenly Father feeds them. And aren't you far more valuable to him than they are? Can all your worries add a single moment to your life?" (Matthew 6:25–27 NLT)

Dr. Frank Newport

DR. FRANK NEWPORT is a Gallup senior scientist. He was Gallup editor in chief from 1990 to 2018 and served as the 2010 to 2011 president of the American Association for Public Opinion Research, the nation's largest and oldest professional association for survey researchers and pollsters. He graduated from Baylor University, from which he received the Distinguished Alumni Award in 2002, and holds a MA and PhD in sociology from the University of Michigan.

Dr. Newport is coauthor of *Words That Matter: How the News and Social Media Shaped the 2016 Presidential Campaign* (2020), coauthor of *Winning the White House 2008: The Gallup Poll, Public Opinion and the Presidency* (2009), author of *Polling Matters—Why Leaders Must Listen to the Wisdom of the People* (2008), coauthor of *The Evangelical Voter*, coeditor of *The Gallup Poll: Public Opinion 2004–2014*, and author of *God Is Alive and Well: The Future of Religion in America* (2012).

Newport has published widely in professional, scholarly, and consumer publications and has contributed thousands of research articles, blogs, videos, podcasts, editorials, and research analyses on Gallup.com, to which he continues to write the *Polling Matters* blog. Frank was founder and cohost of the podcast *Objective Religion*, focused on religion and society, during the 2020 election year.

Over the course of his career as Gallup editor in chief, Dr. Newport made regular appearances on most major television news networks and network programs as well as radio and podcast interviews. Frank pioneered CNN's remote "flash" studio concept, appearing live from Gallup's Princeton studios on CNN US and CNN International. He has been a radio and television announcer, talk-show host, and radio news director. Frank and his wife live and work near Princeton, New Jersey, and have four grown children.

Clayton Crawford's Lasting Impact

IN THE EARLY 1980s our family lived in Bellaire, Texas, an incorporated town surrounded by the city of Houston. Our family attended Bellaire Presbyterian Church. This was largely the decision of my wife, who had been raised in and remained part of the Presbyterian tradition. I myself was deeply enmeshed in the Southern Baptist tradition growing up, son of a Baptist preacher, seminary professor, author and theologian, grandson of a legendary Baptist student leader, and graduate of the world's largest Baptist university. But at this juncture in my life, I was clearly the trailing spouse when it came to religion. My wife was an official member and frequent attender with the children; myself more often than not a non-attender.

The minister of Bellaire Presbyterian left for another pulpit. I barely knew the departed minister and had no particularly memorable contact with him. As happens in these situations, an interim minister arrived, in this instance an older, previously retired gentleman and Presbyterian paster named Clayton Crawford.

The defining moment—one that has been imprinted in my mind ever since—came one day when Rev. Crawford showed up in person on our doorstep at our house in Bellaire. He got right to the point. He was not there to see my wife, the official church member. He was there to see me, the one who at that point was rarely darkening the door of the church. I remember well his looking into my eyes and asking me why I wasn't a member and why I wasn't an active part of the church. He gently probed my thoughts about religion and my religious beliefs and stated directly that he wished I would become an official member and participant in the church life. This was a visit made purely on his own initiative; neither I nor my wife had made any request for a visit or even intimated that a pastoral visit was needed.

The defining moment for me was not so much the manifest issue of my religious history, background, and beliefs nor of the circumstances surrounding being an official member of a church versus being an "asterisk"—a spouse who in the church directory was noted as not being an official member. The defining moment was the fact that this man, Clayton Crawford, had taken a specific and direct interest in me personally and my well-being, faith, and future. The life lesson was based on the stark reality of comparison—the rarity of an instance in which an individual, any individual, takes the time to care about and take a deep personal interest in a person.

Clayton Crawford passed away in the months after his visit, and I did and have remained a more active participant in religious life in the years and decades since. But the life lesson that has become apparent to me and has stuck with me ever since is the gift and power we give to others through the simple gesture of looking them in the eye and indicating a real interest in who they are and what they have to say.

The fact of life is that we humans are mainly interested in ourselves as we move through our time on this mortal coil. In our thoughts and our behavior and very often in our conversations with others, we are concerned with how what is being said affects and relates to ourselves. This leads to the "trigger effect" in conversation. When Person A makes a point or divulges a feeling or relates an anecdote, our main response is more often than not to trigger off of what the person has said to flip the reference to ourselves—how what they said relates to us or how it reminds us of a situation in our own lives or histories. We evince more interest in ourselves, in short, than in the person with whom we are talking.

I'm reminded of two wise insights that have stuck with me over the years. One from the late entrepreneur Mary Kay Ash, who implored her employees to assume that anyone with whom they came in contact was wearing an invisible sign saying, "Make me feel important." And the second the unattributed assertion that the three most important words in the English language are "Tell me more." So many of us are busy with our own concerns and priorities and feelings and beliefs that we simply don't have the time or the inclination to be focused on others. Clayton Crawford helped me understand, to this day, the potential I have in simple interactions to be a positive, life-changing force for others by simply expressing a genuine interest in who they are and what they are doing and feeling.

The Collective Wisdom of the People

I SERVED AS the editor in chief of the Gallup Poll for twenty-eight years, but in reality, I backed into the position and only later came to define it as a moment of realization that changed my life focus from that point on.

Through a set of circumstances, the Houston company in which I was a partner was acquired by a company in Lincoln, Nebraska. The following year that company (Selection Research, Inc) acquired Gallup. A few years after that, the management at Gallup asked me to move to Princeton, New Jersey, to take over leadership of the Gallup Poll. I was happy to do so, but at that point in my career my main focus in life had not been polling or the study of public opinion but social science and the application of social science to the business and political sector. I had spent my years in Houston conducting surveys and marketing research and advising television stations, radio stations, newspapers, and political consultants on how to reach their business objectives. And before that I was an academic, teaching sociology as a scholarly discipline.

But when I moved to Princeton in the new job, I found myself deeply immersed in the world of polling—the use of survey research to measure public opinion and in turn to make the results known to the world and in particular to elected leaders. Polling uses samples to estimate what a large group of people in an underlying population are thinking and feeling about a wide variety of things, including the policies and issues of the day. And the results can, and should, in my opinion, make a real difference in the direction of human society.

In my new position, I began to read the works and writings of the pioneers of public opinion research, and in particular the work of Dr. George Gallup, our company's founder—who died in 1984 and whom I never met or knew (although I got to know his two sons well over the years before their deaths).

The defining moment came as I began to acknowledge and appreciate Dr. Gallup's deep and abiding commitment to the value of collective opinion of all of the people of society—as opposed to the value of the opinions of politicians, ideologues, opinion influencers, and other elites who each claim to have "the truth." Dr. Gallup was well known for his pioneering efforts in using surveys to predict election outcomes, but his basic, underlying interest was in the value of surveys for the guidance of democracy. His book *The Pulse of Democracy,* which I have on my shelf to this day, summarized in its title his view of the role of the people of the country.

This newly recognized focus on the value of the collective opinions of the people of the country changed my orientation to life so much that I ended up writing a book about it myself, and I have emphasized the power of that wisdom in the years since. The lesson learned, in many ways, is a humbling one: the idea that any one person's views and opinions are just that—one person's—and that more often than not, collecting views across a wide spectrum of individuals will yield effective guidance for how and where the society should be moving.

Of course, not everyone agrees with this—another humbling lesson. The US is set up as a representative democracy, which means that elected representatives intervene between the public and government policy making. Some critics argue that they—the representatives—have within their power the capability of serving as trustees of the people and making decisions on their own without recourse to the people who sent them to Washington. Of course, these representatives have to make their decisions on some basis using some criteria, and I believe they are wise to heed the wisdom of both the people they represent and the people of the nation as a whole. I tend to doubt the wisdom of elites or self-anointed thought leaders, or at the least think it appropriate to test wisdom against what the people think and feel.

Another objection to paying attention to the collective views of the people is the assertion that they (that is, the people) are too dumb and ill-informed to have wisdom. That may be true in some instances. Clearly a citizen farmer in Iowa may not be as versed in foreign policy nuances as members of foreign relations committees in the House and Senate. But what the people of the country have that elected representatives do not is highly varied, real-life experiences and experiential knowledge. A waitress, an American Indian, a young struggling actor, a plumber, a farmer, a person struggling to pay the mortgage, cashier, food preparation worker, janitor, lawyer, doctor, and a scientist all have experiences that elected representatives have not. Polling provides the ability to collect the opinions of all these disparate people, collate them, and provide them to our representatives.

My convictions on this score make me at times a rather boring dinner guest, given that I tend to quote what the people think rather than giving personal opinions. But what indeed is the opinion of this one person (me)? Along with this comes the lesson that I not take myself and my opinions too seriously. Of course, this essay is an instance of my expressing my opinions (!), so readers certainty will benefit by putting it in the context of the thoughts of others. In the end, the life lesson learned: all of us have our perspectives and opinions and accumulated wisdom to which attention can and should be profitably paid.

Jan Evans Patterson, MD

DR. PATTERSON IS a native of Fort Worth, Texas. She graduated from Hardin-Simmons University, received her medical degree from McGovern UT Medical School at Houston, and trained in internal medicine at Vanderbilt University Medical Center and in infectious diseases Yale University School of Medicine. She completed a master's in healthcare management at the Harvard School of Public Health. Dr. Patterson recently completed an integrative medicine fellowship at the Andrew Weil Center for Integrative Medicine at University of Arizona.

She has more than thirty years of experience in the practice of infectious diseases, as well as the field of infection prevention, healthcare epidemiology, and quality improvement. She currently practices infectious diseases and integrative medicine at UT Health in San Antonio and is medical director for the Integrative Medicine program at University Health. She is the author of more than 150 scientific publications. She is a past president of the Society for Healthcare Epidemiology of America and has served on the board of directors for the Infectious Diseases Society of America. She has served on the CDC Healthcare Infection Control Practices Advisory Committee.

Dr. Patterson has been a consultant to the South Texas Regional Advisory Council for infectious-diseases emergency preparedness since 2001. She is a part of the COVID-19 response team at UT Health San Antonio, providing consultation and leadership regarding testing, policy, PPE, and patient-care issues. She also has previous pandemic experience, working in Toronto during the 2003 SARS I pandemic and participating in University Health efforts during the 2009 H1N1 pandemic.

Dr. Patterson's book *Breath for the Soul*, using her knowledge of integrative medicine and her passion for healing to encourage people to give self-care, will be released later this year.

She has been married to Thomas Patterson, MD, for thirty-seven years. She is the mother of two sons and two dogs and enjoys gardening and essential oils in her spare time.

A Night in the ICU

AS A FOURTH-YEAR medical student, I looked forward to an elective at a mission hospital in southern India. As soon as I stepped off the plane, I witnessed the crowds, hustle, bustle, and contrast that is India. The ride to the hospital was chaotic, as we weaved in and out around cars and cattle-drawn wagons. I arrived at the hospital grounds to find bright-yellow jacarandas and hot-pink bougainvillea in full bloom at that time of year.

I was grateful to stay at the nearby residence and was welcomed by the medical missionary who lived there. The house was comfortable—except for no hot water. I was glad for the mosquito net, and I tried to ignore the lizard in the bathroom. Well, I wasn't there for comfort anyway. I looked forward to seeing patients in the hospital the next day.

The next morning, I woke up to the *chink, chink, chink* from workers in the rock quarry just behind the house and was anxious to get to the hospital. Even early in the morning, there was a crowd—people of all ages—waiting patiently to be seen in the clinics. In the coming days, I was to see all types of diseases. There were the usual cases of pneumonia, ulcer disease, and heart disease, but also many illnesses we did not usually see in the US—

severe malnutrition, advanced tuberculosis, leprosy, parasitic infections, and cancer presenting at advanced stages.

I learned from the staff how to work in a hospital with routine outages of electricity three times daily and without advanced diagnostic imaging like CT scans or extensive laboratory tests. The patient's story and physical exam were the most important diagnostic steps, and I learned to rely on them much more than I had in my previous medical training.

I took night calls with the staff, who helped me learn how to manage the variety of diseases seen in a mission hospital. They also taught me how to deliver babies, and I gained much more experience with deliveries than I did in my obstetrics rotation at home.

One night call in the intensive-care unit was especially memorable. That day, a farm worker came in after stepping on a nail a few days earlier. He had spasms in his neck and jaw muscles that threatened to close his airway. This disease—tetanus, commonly known as lockjaw—is a disease uncommon in the US due to vaccination. It is caused by a bacterium, *Clostridium tetani*, that is introduced from an object, usually contaminated by soil, and produces a toxin that causes muscle spasms. The spasms can spread to the rest of the body, affecting the respiratory muscles, and the spasms in the neck and throat area can become so severe that it becomes impossible to breathe.

At home, we would treat with tetanus immune globulin to counteract the deadly toxin released from this bacterium. However, this treatment was not available. The wound was cleaned, and unhealthy tissue was removed to eliminate as much of the bacterial contamination as possible. Then the patient was hospitalized, a standard practice in order to provide supportive care. Careful sedation and a quiet environment help to avoid worsening of the spasms. He needed close monitoring and so was admitted to the intensive-care unit.

On that same day, a woman was admitted with a high fever and abdominal pain. She also had a faint rash on the abdomen. These signs and symptoms suggested a very common bacterial infection in the area—typhoid fever. Due to the severity of her infection, she required intravenous antibiotics and was admitted to the intensive-care unit. Even with antibiotics, this infection can take a while to respond. The high fevers from typhoid fever can lead to confusion and delirium, causing the patient to cry out or shout, as this patient did.

A third patient in the small intensive-care unit that night was a heart-attack patient who had sustained a lot of heart damage, resulting in an unstable blood pressure. He required intravenous medicine to support his heart and circulation. At home, we would have used an automated IV pump in order to make small and accurate adjustments to the medicine. At the mission hospital, we were only able to turn the medicine up and down by hand, sometimes resulting in wide swings in blood pressure. This medication required frequent monitoring and adjustment through the night.

So, in the intensive-care unit that night, we were very

busy trying to give careful sedation to the tetanus patient while also trying to control the delirious shouts of the typhoid patient that could exacerbate the spasms of the tetanus patient. And we were repeatedly adjusting the intravenous medicine to support blood pressure in the heart-attack patient as best we could.

As dawn came and other staff took over, I realized this experience made me acutely aware of the privilege of technically sophisticated and safer health care in the US. I was also mindful of God's spiritual presence with us that strengthened our vigilance and helped us provide the best care available during that night.

I was to call on this experience many times in the future. During my medical residency training and then my medical faculty years, I recalled that whatever illnesses and difficult situations in treating patients, there were none more challenging than that memorable night in the intensive-care unit and that God was by my side.

I was also to reflect on this lesson in my personal life. There was a time when I was recovering from cancer surgery while dealing with my dad's dementia and my brother's terminal condition after my mother passed away. At the same time, we were grieving our younger son's death. It was overwhelming.

I called on God's promise that was one of my parents' favorites: "Trust in the LORD with all your heart and lean not on your own understanding; in all your ways submit to him, and he will make your paths straight" (Proverbs 3:5–6 NIV).

There are times in life when we have problems that

appear insurmountable. We do not understand why it is all happening or what path to follow. We can, however, call on the strength, guidance, and comfort that can only come from God and rest in the peace that only He can provide.

Paul reminds us, "Do not be anxious about anything, but in every situation, by prayer and petition, with thanksgiving, present your requests to God. And the peace of God, which transcends all understanding, will guard your hearts and your minds in Christ Jesus" (Philippians 4:6–7 NIV).

Protection in a Pandemic

IN 2002 AN unknown severe respiratory illness appeared in China. It was spread from person to person and had a significant mortality rate. It was not influenza, and further investigation showed it to be a novel coronavirus, similar to the already described coronaviruses that were among the causes of the common cold. The disease was much more serious than the common cold, however, causing hospitalizations and even deaths. The disease was acute and could progress very quickly. Because of these characteristics, the syndrome was called Severe Acute Respiratory Syndrome (SARS), and the causative virus was called SARS-associated coronavirus (SARS-CoV, now known as SARS-CoV-1).

The disease quickly spread to twenty-nine countries and regions and was declared a pandemic. More than eight thousand cases and 774 deaths were reported. Most affected countries were in Asia, but the disease spread from Asia to Toronto, and that city had a four-month, two-stage outbreak of SARS, with 250 cases and thirty-eight deaths, including deaths in health-care workers. The overall death rate was 10 percent and greater than 50 percent in the elderly. North America was relatively spared with the US having few cases and no deaths.

There was no specific therapy for SARS; it was eventually controlled with infection control and public-health measures, including quarantine and isolation. There have been no cases of SARS since 2004.

Of course, SARS was the harbinger of COVID-19, which has proven to be a much larger problem, causing more than five hundred million identified cases and six million identified deaths worldwide. More than one million deaths have occurred in the US alone. SARS-CoV-2 is the virus causing COVID-19. Instead of being controlled in a two-year period as SARS was, COVID-19 has been a pandemic for more than two years. The reason for the differences in these two pandemics is not fully explained, but the initial virus causing 2003 SARS was less transmissible and more deadly. This may be because it is primarily an infection of the lungs and lower respiratory tract. COVID-19 is more transmissible and less deadly, probably because it starts as an upper-respiratory-tract infection. It is when it spreads to the lungs and causes an overactive immune response that it becomes deadly. The initial SARS outbreak in 2003 gave investigators of the mRNA vaccine time to begin developing a strategy for a coronavirus vaccine, namely to target the spike protein that lets the virus enter the cell.

My story occurred during the SARS 2003 pandemic. Toronto was one of the areas hardest hit by that pandemic. The second wave of the pandemic was primarily due to transmission of the virus in hospitals—among patients, visitors, and health-care workers. There was no vaccine developed and no specific treatment, so there was much attention to infection control measures.

At that time, infectious-disease doctors who also had experience and expertise in hospital infection control were scarce in Canada. Most Toronto hospitals did not have them. Hospitalized patients and health-care workers were getting sick, and some health-care workers saw their colleagues die of this disease. The infectious-diseases community and Canadian public-health officials implemented infection-control measures, and they also wanted more expertise to make sure they were doing all that was needed. They called upon members of the Society for Healthcare Epidemiology of America (SHEA), our professional society of infectious-diseases physicians specializing in infection control, to come and work in Toronto hospitals to ensure maximal precautions were in place.

Several other colleagues and I were called upon to go, and we felt an obligation to help Toronto. As an infectious-diseases physician, we accept a certain amount of risk with the job. However, most of the time we have the right protective equipment and vaccinations or treatments to counteract diseases to which we are exposed. Not so with SARS in 2003. However, I felt called to go and discussed the situation with my family. My husband, another infectious-diseases physician with different expertise, and my two sons understood and were supportive of my trip.

As I sat in the airport waiting to get on the plane to Toronto, I saw headlines of more SARS deaths in Canada. Although I had felt called to go, I began to have doubts. I opened the daily devotion on my phone, and these are the verses I read:

> Those who live in the shelter of the Most High
> will find rest in the shadow of the Almighty.
> This I declare about the Lord:
> He alone is my refuge, my place of safety;
> he is my God, and I trust him.
> For he will rescue you from every trap
> and protect you from deadly disease.
> (Psalms 91:1–3 NLT)

I kept reading the psalmist's words.

> If you make the Lord your refuge,
> if you make the Most High your shelter,
> no evil will conquer you;
> no plague will come near your home.
> For he will order his angels
> to protect you wherever you go.
> They will hold you up with their hands
> so you won't even hurt your foot on a stone.
> (Psalms 91:9–12 NLT)

I was amazed that the exact words I needed to hear were in that day's devotional. I took it as God's assurance that I was doing the right thing and He would keep me safe. I felt held and protected.

The next few weeks in Toronto went well, and the hospital where I served was grateful for our help. We learned a lot, including policies and practices that would help us in our own hospitals during the 2009 H1N1 influenza pandemic and of course in the recent COVID-19 pandemic.

The lesson I learned was that if I am following God's call, He will provide assurance and protection for what He wants to accomplish through me. At the beginning of the COVID-19 pandemic, of course there was no vaccine or treatment. We were fortunate to have the appropriate equipment, although we knew that it was not 100 percent protective. Nevertheless, I was able to do my job consulting on COVID-19 patients and examining them when needed because I knew I was following my calling.

Wherever peril lurks in life, I can seek God's calling and feel an amazing assurance and protection because of His promises.

Dr. Jack Robbins

JACK ROBBINS GREW up in rural North Carolina. His dad was a tenant farmer with a seventh-grade education. Jack was saved and dramatically changed as a senior in high school and baptized as a Baptist the next year. He spent two years at Campbell College in Buies Creek, NC, then completed his degree and graduated from Samford University in Birmingham, AL. During his senior year at Samford, he began pastoring at Enon Baptist church, Centreville, AL.

He received master's and doctorate degrees from Southwestern Baptist Theological Seminary in Ft. Worth, TX. His most notable pastorates were FBC Sulphur Springs, TX, and Immanuel Baptist, Duncan, OK. and the planting of Open Door Church, Raleigh, NC. For forty years, he has led LOVEM Ministries, a nonprofit 501(c)(3) organization of ministers and ministries. Contributions from his pen include articles for denominational papers and local newspapers as well as missionary publications.

He writes, "Like John Newton, I received God's 'Amazing Grace that saved a wretch like me!' Today I'm praising God my salvation is lasting and eternal. By the guidance and grace of God I've served the Lord imperfectly but faithfully for sixty-two years and have had the joy of ministering in churches as youth minister and senior pastor in Alabama, Oklahoma, Texas, and North Carolina, church planter, evangelist, missionary, professor (SEBTS), and associate pastor. I've ministered in forty-six nations including Pakistan, Cuba, Brazil, North Korea, China, and Israel, all fifty states and one hundred counties in North Carolina."

Jesus Loves Me. This I Know!

MEMORY IS A divine gift! Our memory bank grows, but some memories become monumental as they contribute to the whole of our lives.

In 1947 Clarence E. McCartney, evangelical Presbyterian pastor, published his *Great Nights of the Bible,* one of his about fifty books. It included sixteen nights. I have one especially "great night."

The date was April 6, 1960. The place, the parking lot of Ellerbe (NC) High School. In less than two months I expected to receive my high-school diploma and begin life as a student at Campbell College.

Our high school provided an elective class in Bible. I chose to take two years, one under Miss Catherine Holcombe and one under Miss Frances Thompson. In the spring members of the Bible Club, students from their classes, visited sponsoring area churches who provided support for these teachers and presented a program on the Bible class experience. After one of these evenings, I requested some time with Miss Thompson to discuss a question.

My boyhood dream was to play professional baseball beyond high school. A part of this dream was to win a state championship with our high-school baseball team.

My spiritual experience to that point involved the idea that if I did something for God, He would do something for me. Every day we had a game I read a chapter in the Bible and prayed to win our baseball game. It occurred to me that if another player on the opposing team was praying the same prayer, I was putting God in an impossible position. And if the game had to end in a tie, everyone loses. So, my question to Miss Thompson that night was, "Is it wrong to pray to win a baseball game?"

Sharing a testimony of her high-school experience when God answered her prayer for a certain young man to ask her to the prom, she assured me that God cares about the little things in our lives as well as the big things. In the course of our discussion, she posed the question, "Why did Jesus die?"—a very simple question for a high-school senior with a bad case of "senioritis." But I did not respond immediately. God was giving me a vision of my future, a picture of Jesus dying on the cross, body broken, bruised, bloody and torn, hanging against a clear-blue sky, looking straight into my eyes and saying, "I'm doing this for you! I'm dying that you may live, love, and follow Me." I knew! Yes, Jesus Loves Me! This I Know!

I was flooded by a sense of connection and claim upon my life, of purpose, meaning. All to Him I surrendered: my sins, my foolishness, my future. I saw the way and the truth.

I had been confirmed in the Methodist Church when I was twelve. I had walked the aisle in a Baptist Church with a friend when I was fourteen. I had gone forward in a Billy Graham crusade in Charlotte when I was sixteen. But after a week or two in each of those instances I had fallen back into my old patterns. A real lasting change had not occurred.

But something drastically changed in my spirit that night. On my bedroom floor I vowed to live for Christ even if it meant death. I'd do anything He wanted me to do, go anywhere He wanted me to go, say anything He wanted me to say. And I've never looked back. I live to tell the story! This was the "great night" of my soul!

Creation of an Unbreakable Three-Fold Cord

KING SOLOMON'S WISDOM declared, "The man who finds a wife finds a treasure, and he receives favor from the LORD" (Proverbs 18:22 NLT). This is how God revealed His treasure for me.

I was a beginning sophomore at Campbell College (now University) in Buies Creek, North Carolina, just after I had been baptized as a Baptist, leaving my Methodist roots. In a Sunday-morning worship service at Buies Creek First Baptist Church, a youthful, blued-eyed blond among the gray-haired ladies in the choir captured my attention.

A few weeks previously when I had shared a devotional message in our College Baptist Student Union on Sunday evening, this same high-school senior from the choir was present and had heard something that captured her imagination.

I was living in the home of Charles B. Howard beside the church at the time. I asked Barry Howard, his son, to identify the conspicuous young choir member. "That's Ginnie Page!" he said. "Would you like to meet her?"

"Yes, I would!" was my quick response.

Barry soon found an opportunity to introduce Ginnie

and me in the Buies Creek High School gym one evening after the girls' basketball game. That night we had our very first date! We drove to nearby Lillington to dine on hamburgers and Cokes, and then I took her home.

We dated several times, but I had made plans to transfer to Samford University in Birmingham, Alabama, for my junior year. We stayed in touch from time to time, and Ginnie came with the Howards to my ordination into the ministry at the First Baptist Church of Ellerbe, North Carolina, at the Christmas break in 1963. A year later she accompanied my family to my graduation in Birmingham.

Upon graduation I went to Oklahoma as a summer missionary with the Home Mission Board and decided to attend Southwestern Baptist Theological Seminary in Fort Worth, Texas. In 1964 at Christmas Ginnie came to Fort Worth to see her Aunt Bessie and me. By then I was pastoring my second church up in Duncan, Oklahoma. Thanks to the generous hospitality of a deacon's family in the Gatlin Baptist Church there, Ginnie had a comfortable week's visit with me and the church. After a number of letters back and forth, it was decision time for us. My life with Christ was such that I was willing, like Paul, to remain single, and I had seriously considered it. I wanted to be fully focused on God's call and direction with no distractions or missteps. Some fear gripped my heart as I considered engagement and marriage. I could not afford to make any mistakes.

In my dorm room at Southwestern Seminary, I got down on my knees and fervently prayed. I confessed to

God my uncertainty about marriage to anyone. I prayed, "O Lord, reveal to me your will. Give me a word of assurance if I am to ask Ginnie to marry me."

Feelings can create uncertainty—yes? No? Not sure! I did something I'd never done before and have done only once since. I opened the Bible while on my knees with eyes closed and said, "Lord, reveal to me Your will." Upon inspiration, not knowing what book, chapter, nor verse my finger had landed on, I looked down and read, "Can two walk together, except they be agreed?" (Amos 3:3 KJV)

Believing that you need two or three witnesses to establish truth, I took another step. Humbly praying, again I opened my Bible and put my finger on another verse, which happened to be in the Gospel of Matthew. "As he considered this, an angel of the Lord appeared to him in a dream. 'Joseph, Son of David,' the angel said, 'do not be afraid to take Mary as your wife'" (Matthew 1:20 NLT). This spiritual experience confirmed to me that Ginnie Page and I were to become husband and wife! This became reality on June 26, 1965, at the Buies Creek First Baptist church at 4:00 p.m. When sharing this with one brother, he quipped, "Why didn't you marry Mary?"

That New Year's Day in Duncan, Oklahoma, we started a tradition that extends to the present. We have spent almost every January 1 with that deacon and his family. Since his son died in a diabetic coma on his eighteenth birthday, our children claimed them as grandparents, and they have been like family.

On June 26, 2022, we will celebrate our fifty-seventh

anniversary with four adult children and nine grandchildren. Our cord of three strands was formed. We have walked hand in hand and heart to heart, following the Lord Jesus Christ.

Camille Bishop Simmons

CAMILLE SIMMONS IS a graduate of Nashville High School, Ouachita Baptist University, and Southwestern Baptist Theological Seminary (SWBTS). She did doctoral studies in music at SWBTS and the University of Michigan.

In 1969 Camille married James M. Simmons (1940–2018) and served by his side as a pastor's wife for forty-eight years. She and Jim also served as appointed missionaries with the International Mission Board and the North American Mission Board.

Camille served as coordinator for ministry missions with San Antonio Baptist Association from November 1990 to September 2006. Through her leadership, San Antonio became a pilot site in the nation for the development of Christian Women's Job Corps, founded by

Woman's Missionary Union. She was active with her community in disaster preparedness and response and was the faith community representative at Incident Command during hurricanes Katrina and Rita.

Camille gave oversight to the development of One by One Ministries and was executive director of One by One for eight years (September 2006 to May 2014). She received the Beall award for Excellence in Community Ministries from the North American Mission Board and the Creativity in Missions Development award from the Baptist Foundation of Texas.

Camille is now married to Dr. Ernest Izard. Her son Dr. Jim Simmons serves as a minister of music. In semiretirement, she teaches voice and piano at the Mount Pleasant Music Studio, is active in her church, and spends time with her five grandchildren.

My Remedial Experience in Trusting God

WALK AND FRET. Walk and fret. I was walking around in circles on the high-school stadium track before going to work that spring morning. I walked and I fretted. How had I gotten to such a spiritual, emotional, and mental state?

Over a year prior we had found out that San Antonio was going to host the Olympic Festival. As coordinator of ministry missions for a large association of churches, I became active in planning and preparation for ministries that would be offered during this event. I enjoy networking and teamwork, and it was a joy to work with local, state, and national organizations to see these ministry ideas become reality.

The scope of these preparations along with my normal work made it clear that I needed someone to become head of the Olympic Festival ministries team. I was thrilled when I was able to hire a wonderful lady who was a leader and a smart, vibrant, extravert organizer. She did a great job working with the representatives of multiple agencies and ministries. Together they formed teams that would ensure the provision of ministries at each of the Olympic Festival events sites, including hosting the visiting athletes.

One of the big projects was working with the American Bible Society to produce ten thousand Bibles for distribution during the festival. Funds from three different sources made it possible for us to get a beautiful design for the cover of the paperback Bibles as well as for their production and shipping. The design was named "Lift the Light." These beautiful paperback Bibles, seven thousand New Testaments and three thousand entire Bibles, were in the Contemporary English Version.

As with every project, some things go smoothly and some things don't. At first, we were told that no one would have access to any of the athletes. Their housing would be at local university campuses. We laughed and rejoiced the day that a Christian athletic organization was asked to be the host for the Olympic Festival athletes!

Then came the day when our wonderful Olympic Festival ministries team leader found out that her husband had terminal cancer. She had to resign her position. She had done a fantastic job already, and the large majority of the ministries were prepared, ready, and in place for the summer starting date. The preparation team continued to function well.

There was one major ministry that was not planned—one I felt was an important crown jewel of all of the ministries that would be done for those ten days of the Olympic Festival. We did not yet have the location of our downtown welcome center.

Thus it was that I was walking in circles around that track and fretting about the location of that downtown welcome center being needed and needed fast! As I finished my laps and started walking home, the Lord spoke to me. He told me He was the Sovereign God and then asked if I thought He could handle this welcome center location! Breathing became difficult. I stopped walking and proceeded to ask His forgiveness for my thoughtless lack of trust in Him. I declared to Him that I knew He would provide everything related to this welcome center.

Right after staff prayer meeting that morning, I decided to drive around downtown San Antonio and pray as I drove. What hit me smack in the face was that there were so many parking lots downtown. I drove up to the parking lot right beside the historic Alamo.

I asked the attendant if I could have the phone number of the owner of these parking lots.

He asked, "What do you plan to do?"

I told him.

He said, "I know just the person for you to call." He gave me the number, and I headed back to the office, praying all the way. Back in my office, I prayed before I called that phone number. When I called, a secretary answered. I had played phone tag numerous times and was prepared for that scenario. I was shocked when she said, "He's right here. Just a moment."

Immediately the gentleman with whom I wanted to speak answered and asked how he could help me. I requested that we be able to rent some of his parking spaces for ministries related to the Olympic Festival. He asked me what we wanted to place in those spaces and what we planned to do. So I explained that we would have a disaster relief trailer, a welcome booth, and folding chairs. I told him we wanted to serve sno-cones, do fun activities, and hand out Bibles.

I was prepared to give added compelling information when He said that of course we could have the spaces. After I regained my composure, I asked that since they owned the parking lots, would he like to tell me which spaces they would allow us to rent. His reply was that he would never do that. He told me to go choose the location and however many spaces we wanted and that they were ours for the festival at no charge!

And so it was that I went from walking and fretting to rejoicing and thanking God for His provision as we set up that welcome center right on the main route between the Alamo Dome and the Alamo. A disaster-relief volunteer set up the trailer and helped man the welcome center the entire ten days. A wonderful summer missionary manned the booth and scheduled and supervised the volunteers who served there.

Thousands of visitors from Maine to Mexico came to the welcome center. They got sno-cones, Bibles, plan of salvation bracelets, and the gospel was shared with them. Some of them made decisions to follow Christ. Employees from businesses on the River Walk came and requested Bibles for their employee Bible study groups. Then letters from the county jail started arriving. It seems that some of the Bibles made their way there. How I rejoiced when I read their thank-you letters. Many of them told me they had never been able to understand the Bible. Because they now had a Contemporary English

Version of the Bible, they could understand what they were reading. They were thrilled to be able to learn more about God! They thanked me profusely for making it possible for them to get those Bibles.

I had walked with my Lord from my early youth. The decisions in my life were based on my desire to serve Him with all my heart. I was a pastor's wife and a missionary. But in my hard work to see ministries done, I had put my focus on accomplishing important things instead of communing with my loving Father. I had let myself get too busy to seek Him and His ways. I will forever be grateful for His loving, gracious response to me and for His awesome provision. May I always seek Him first!

Let the Children Come to Me

I WAS ON my knees scrubbing floors. There aren't many parsonages left anymore, but we lived in one in San Antonio, Texas. I don't know who chose the flooring for the kitchen and family room, but they really liked grooves. They must have thought it gave floors character. Well, those grooves were testing my character! As I worked hard to get those floors clean, I prayed earnestly. I reminded the Lord of what He already knew. I trusted Him early. I surrendered to missions early. My life focus was to serve Him. I was on a team of five who started a new church when I was sixteen. (It's still alive.) In my teen years I taught vacation Bible school in rural churches in the summer. I was a college and seminary graduate. I was a pastor's wife and a former missionary. I wanted with all my heart to serve Him.

At the time of this plea to the Lord, I had been at home for a year with my oldest son, Mark, who had contracted Chronic Fatigue Immune Deficiency Syndrome. His health was improving enough that it was possible that I might be able to serve somewhere in a part-time position. I passionately asked the Lord to lead me to what He had for me next. Then I added a P.S. "Please, Lord, I don't want to work at Burger King!"

Two weeks later I received a call from Dr. Lewis Lee, director of missions for San Antonio Baptist Association. He asked me to consider joining their staff in a missions outreach capacity. I told him I needed to ask my family, and I needed four weeks to pray about it. My family gave me enthusiastic support. As I prayed for four weeks, the Lord spoke to me over and over about the need to minister to families.

I met with Dr. Lee and told him I was honored to serve in the part-time position so long as I was considered for the full-time position. He hired me and I became coordinator of ministry missions for San Antonio Baptist Association (November 1990 to September 2006). I had the privilege of working with over two hundred churches facilitating ministries awareness, training, and support that would help them reach outside their four walls to meet people at the point of their needs, minister to those needs, and share Christ with them. It was exciting work, and I loved every minute of it.

I worked with leaders who represented several different ministries. We formed a ministry-missions team. Among the ministries represented on that team were Hunger, Literacy, Health, Restorative Justice, Christian Women's Job Corps, and Family Ministries.

I visited with teachers, policemen, city officials, and judges from across San Antonio. Their response to my question of what they felt was important was always the same answer: to teach parents how to parent their children.

In 1994 our association became involved in what was

called Mega Focus Cities Strategic Planning. The goal of the strategic planning was to discover who our churches needed to be to better reach our city.

During that year we met with focus groups for brainstorming sessions and prayer. These groups consisted of church staff members, our ministry missions team, ministry volunteers, and representatives from our institutions. We looked at the needs of San Antonio. As we did, ministering to families was always at the forefront of my prayers.

In November of 1995 over two hundred pastors, spouses, staff, associational staff, and state and national representatives met in New Braunfels, Texas, for two days of strategic planning. When all was said and done, ministering to families was chosen the number one priority for the association. I was amazed, thrilled, and challenged. I immediately began meeting with our focus groups. In just weeks we had developed a pie chart of family ministries that churches should be doing. From that pie chart we realized that to mentor expectant and new parents was the most critically needed ministry. We discussed how that would be done. I attended a thirty-two-hour training done by a new-parent mentoring organization. The curriculum was good. However, it was secular, and I found out they would not train church-based volunteers to provide that curriculum to young families.

I called the leader of one of our ministry partners and said that we needed to create a new curriculum that is specifically made for churches. We received grant funding from two of our partners to develop this ministry. I asked an early-childhood development specialist and director of a child development center in Austin to write the curriculum. She did a brilliant, marvelous job and worked with a graphic artist and editor to give the curriculum a winning format. The curriculum produced has been praised by physicians and educators alike and is still in use today.

The curriculum author, the graphic artist and editor, and I worked side by side for ten years to give birth to this new ministry. One by One Ministries trains volunteers from local churches to mentor expectant and new parents, share Christ with them, and link them to a local church. Our goal is that babies of participant parents have their best opportunity to thrive with godly, healthy parental love and grow up free of abuse and neglect. One by One trains our mentors to share the gospel with participant families. One by One is currently being implemented in churches in Memphis, Dallas, and San Antonio. There are many stories of parents who have trusted in Christ and are raising healthy babies.

When I was scrubbing those floors and asking for a new opportunity to serve Him, I had absolutely no idea of how much the Lord had planned! His ways are beyond our comprehension!

The greatest needed ministry in our nation today is to reach expectant/new parents with the gospel, disciple them to become committed Christ followers, and mentor them in godly healthy parenting. My heart cry and prayer is for these new generations because they are the future of our families, churches, and our nation. I pray you will join me in this prayer: let the little children come to Jesus!

Dr. Larry Williams

BORN IN RURAL Arkansas, Dr. Williams sensed a call to enter ministry. He entered Ouachita Baptist University in Arkadelphia, AR, where he received his BA and MA degrees. He completed his master of divinity degree from Southwestern Baptist Theological Seminary and then completed his ThD in philosophy of religion. He later did further studies in psychology and converted his ThD to a PhD.

As he pastored four churches in Arkansas and Texas over a twenty-year period, his pastoral counseling during those years evolved into the ministry and profession of psychotherapy and marital counseling.

Dr. Williams continues to serve as a pastoral counselor and marriage and family counselor with over thirty years of experience in his private practice. He is a clinical member of the American Association of Marriage and Family Therapists and published author of *Look at You: Essentials for Taking Good Care of Yourself and Relationships.*

He and his wife, Linda, have three children and seven grandchildren. As a lifetime avid exerciser, he enjoys playing golf and riding horses. He continues to work and is presently writing two novels and a screenplay. At eighty-four years of age, his plan is to live to be one hundred years old.

Website: FamilyLifeTherapy.org

Deciding on the Best Road to Travel

The roads that led to my defining moment were crooked, winding, country gravel roads. After my mother had an attack of agoraphobia while playing the piano at the church, she never attended again. My father did not attend, so I had to walk to church. Because we moved every two years, sometimes the gravel or dirt road would be as much as mile. Mother would always say how proud of me she was, so I tried to go as often as I could.

One of those country roads was to the Spring Grove Baptist Church near my grandparents' country home. Sometimes we would go to visit early Sunday morning. Their house, with a wraparound porch, multiple chimneys, and shingle roof, sat on a high hill among huge trees. It was like a setting in a movie with its barns, garden, orchard, and all kinds of farm animals.

The church was a quarter of a mile walk, which I walked gladly. I remember the hand fans with a picture of the Christ we used to keep ourselves cool or fight off wasps. But what I remember most was the singing of "The Old Rugged Cross" and the sermons that helped shape my early faith. Those experiences led to my defining moment.

There were several different roads, but they all led to

churches that ushered me to my defining decision. When I was twelve, we lived in the country on Bard Road. I would walk the gravel or muddy road to the North Side Baptist Church where my faith continued to grow.

Bard Road was the same road that gave me great fear on dark nights, causing me to run home if services got late. One night I decided to walk slowly and trust God to protect me from hobos since I had to cross railroad tracks. As I walked, a calm came over me. Even though it was pitch dark with huge trees on both sides of the road, I had no fear.

Not long after that night's experience, I was walking to church one Sunday morning. I was somewhere between my home and the railroad tracks when I sensed a voice in my mind. I kept hearing that voice saying, "I want you to preach. I want you to preach." Over the next six years I kept thinking about that morning walk and that insistent voice.

So, one night in October of 1956, I drove my '49 Ford to the parsonage. When my pastor, Jerry Autry, came to the door, before I said a word, he said, "Larry, I think I know what you want; let's go over to the church."

We went into a Sunday-school room where I sat down on a cold metal chair shaking all over. I told him that I thought God was calling me to preach. He replied that I was on my own with that decision. Then he looked at me and asked, "What are you going to do?"

Through a trembling body and with a shaky voice, I said, "I'm going to do it." A warm calm came over me. I relaxed and felt great. This was the defining moment in my life. A moment based on a decision that changed the rest of my life. In fact, all defining moments are based on a decision.

The road then took me away from Arkansas State where I was majoring in art to Ouachita Baptist College where I majored in religion. The next road for me was to Texas to Southwestern Seminary, then on to pastorates and ministry-related work.

Life is totally determined by what we believe about God, the world we live in, and who we are. Everything we believe requires a decision. While indecision is a form of a decision, indecision creates one of the highest levels of anxiety. That anxiety can lead to depression. Good decisions can open the door to everything good about this life.

Though I've had many since that night in the First Baptist Church of Paragould, Arkansas, it was the best of all my defining moments. What joy I have in traveling the road of life with a loving God, who created all there is, including me, and with a love for myself and others. That kind of living exceeds any other possible life.

The Power of Encouragement

WHEN I FOLLOWED the road to Ouachita Baptist University, I expected to make straight As as an obligation to God. I failed miserably and felt like I had failed God. At the time, I did not know I was dyslexic and had ADD. I knew that reading and focusing were difficult. I sought help with reading courses and counseling from my professors. They were sympathetic but offered no help.

I had made terrible grades in high school and barely graduated, and I was put on probation after my first semester in Arkansas State. So, I guess I was expecting a miracle since I had followed God's lead. I felt shame.

One night under a full moon I went to the middle of the football field, fell prostrate, cried, and screamed to God to forgive me. I went from there to my political science professor's home. Having been blinded by shrapnel in the war made him more understanding. He invited me in and offered me wonderful support. However, my studies did not improve.

When we signed up for our college courses, we went to the library where we picked up a report card and carried it to the professor whose class we were signing up for. I was signing up for a course in logic with a professor of philosophy, Ms. Raspberry. She looked at me and said, "Larry, I'm sure you will make an A in this course." I turned and walked away with a big smile. For the first time I felt someone believed in my ability to succeed—something I never believed for myself. What a defining moment!

I not only made an A in that course, but I started making As in my other courses. Because of my success, I was able to get into the master's program in American society and thought. The door was opened, and with determination I went on to complete the MDiv and the PhD and post-graduate work in psychology.

In the movie *Zorba the Greek*, when Zorba's boss asked him for something because he believed in him, Zorba broke into an exuberant dance—a dance of celebration of life and the joy of having someone who believed in him. When someone believes in you, it's time to celebrate and dance to the good life.

There are many great stories of encouragers in the Bible. Jesus had close friends who were encouragers to him. Barnabas was a great encourager to the apostle Paul. He guided Paul by spending time with him and letting Paul observe him with new believers at Antioch (see Acts 11), church leaders (see Acts 13), and nonbelievers in their first missionary journey. He even defended Paul from the critics who knew what Paul had been. Encouragement has produced defining moments that have changed history.

What God believes about us is more important than what we believe about God. I think God created us for the same reason we have babies—to have someone to love. We know what God believes about us: "For God so loved the world..." (John 3:16 NIV). Believing that God loves you unconditionally makes it possible for you to love yourself. It is impossible to love yourself too much as long as you love everyone else the same. There is no greater encouragement than love.

Encouragement from godly people through the years has created many defining moments for me. I have received Christmas cards from Ms. Raspberry for years now with notes about what was going on in her life. I'm also hearing from God on a regular basis. God is doing well, and so am I.

Dr. George W. (Bill) Nichols

BILL NICHOLS HOLDS a MDiv and PhD from Southwestern Baptist Theological Seminary, where he taught Christian philosophy, apologetics, evangelism, and world religions. After teaching at the seminary, he began his pastoral ministry as the senior pastor of three churches until he was called to help found ACTS (American Christian Television System), the nation's first faith and family television network representing the country's mainline denominations. He went on to found Kaleidoscope Television Network, the first cable television channel featuring health and disability programming. The channel later became the Hallmark Channel.

Bill has received numerous television, communications, and faith-related recognitions and awards: the

Barbara Jordan Award, James Brady Award, Juvenile Diabetes International Special Service Award, the Religion in American Life Board Award, and the Inter-Faith Network Council Award.

Bill is the author of four made-for-television movies, numerous Bible and discipleship booklets, and three books, including *Healthy Faith: A Strategic Lifestyle Plan to Transform Your Head, Heart and Hands; Devotions for a Healthy Faith: Get to Know God through His 66 Books*; and *Digging Deeper: Exploring the Original Meaning of 30 Key Bible Words*.

Bill also enjoys painting oil portraits, landscapes, and still-life subjects in a classical realism style. He and his wife, Phyllis, live in the Texas Hill Country where they enjoy spending time with their two married daughters and three grandchildren, writing, painting, traveling, and continuing to do Kingdom work.

Website: HealthyFaith.net
Facebook: Bill Nichols
Twitter: billnichols42

Have You Ever Milked a Cow?

I WAS EIGHT the first time I visited my Granddaddy Nichols on his farm in Virginia. Granddaddy lived ten miles from the nearest paved road. When we turned off the highway on to a red-clay makeshift road winding through the hills, I knew I was not only a long way from my home in my tourist town of Pompano Beach, Florida, but I was a long way from everything familiar. It seems I was in for a few surprises.

I had never stayed in a house without electricity. When the sun went down, Granddaddy announced it was time for all God's children to go to bed. I wondered who in the world went to bed so early, but Daddy had told me I was to go along with everything Granddaddy said because we were his guests, and he did things a little differently than we did. So, off to bed I went.

Another surprise: I had never been in a house without indoor plumbing. So, in the middle of the first night when I needed to make my regular trip to the bathroom, I remembered the outhouse was about fifty yards down the hill. I could hear Daddy saying, "You can't miss it. By the way, watch out for snakes."

Thanks to the moonlight, the one-seat tiny outhouse was easy to find. I had never heard the sounds of so many creatures as I made my way, and I imagined they were all watching and waiting for me. When I opened the creaky, old, homemade outhouse door, I peeked in to see if I could spot any snakes. When I decided all was clear, I eased in and left the door open for the moonlight. But it was still dark and so cold that it didn't take me long to get back to the house.

The next morning when Granddaddy woke me up, it was still dark. I learned that he rose every morning at four o'clock to feed the animals and milk the cows before breakfast. I had always taken for granted that people got their milk from the grocery store. It never occurred to me that some people actually milked their own cows. One thing was certain: I had never seen anybody milk a cow. And I had no idea of how to do it. So, naturally, that's the job Granddaddy gave me.

That first morning before daybreak, he handed me the milk bucket and told me to go on out to the barn and milk the cows. I was frightened and didn't think I could do it. So, I told him, "Grandaddy, it's dark out there. I don't know how to milk a cow. And besides, what if there are snakes in that barn?"

Granddaddy put his hand on my shoulder and said, "Wait here." He went out to the barn and returned shortly. "Bill, you can relax now. You don't need to be afraid anymore. I've checked everything out. There are no snakes in the barn, and I turned the light on. And I'll be right by your side all the time to show you what to do. How's that?"

You guessed it. I had a great time milking my first

cow. And in addition to that, our whole family had fresh milk for breakfast because I trusted my granddaddy and did my job. As unspiritual as that experience seemed at the time, for decades it has been one of those defining moments in my life that taught me some great spiritual lessons.

Many times when I have faced some unfamiliar and frightening situations, I remember what happened that morning in Granddaddy's barn. That experience taught me that when I face such times I should remember that my heavenly Father has already scouted things out and has things ready. He has already checked for snakes and turned on the lights. He walks alongside me all the way.

Our Father always does His part in our journey. Hard times are not new to Him. No matter how scary they are to us, they are not scary at all to Him because nothing is impossible for Him, and He's been handling folks' fears from the beginning of time. I also learned from that defining moment that God has a character-building lesson for me in every unfamiliar circumstance. Those times are building my faith muscles—believing my Father tells the truth and depending on Him as I leave the safety of my home and head for the barn.

Although fear is still a powerful emotion, I found that if I don't take control of my fears, they will take control of every part of me. And they'll cause me to miss out on some wonderful things God has planned for me—a meaningful relationship with Him and others, a fulfilling purpose, a deep inner peace, and many enjoyable adventures and exciting opportunities. Faith is risky, but it's always worth it.

When you and I face something that we think could be embarrassing or dangerous, our minds produce feelings of fear, stress, anxiety, or worry. I've discovered that we don't have to allow those feeling to control us. God wants to help us and has the answer for how we can overcome any fear.

Before writing this, I thought it would be interesting to see what answers others give to one of the most often asked questions on the Internet: "How can I overcome my fears?" Would you believe Google found 3,350,000 articles on the subject? Some answers were helpful, but honestly, far too many were laughable. So, I returned to the Bible and found the answer our heavenly Father has been giving people for centuries.

When God's chosen people gazed wishfully across the valley at the unfamiliar and dangerous Promised Land, those people asked the same kind of questions that went through my heart that early morning at my Granddaddy's farm: "What should I do? I'm afraid to go in. Should I stay where it's safe and tell my Father I just can do it?"

Some of God's strong, bright leaders looked over the situation and recommended, "Don't do it. It's too risky. Your enemies are too strong." But God gave them and Joshua, their new leader, the same answer He has always given people paralyzed by their fears, "Do not be afraid or discouraged, for the LORD will personally go ahead of you. He will be with you; he will neither fail you nor abandon you" (Deuteronomy 31:8 NLT).

Sounds too simple, doesn't it? Well, it *is* simple, but it's not easy. Faith is tough at first. Like most things, the more we practice it, the easier it gets. When you are threatened by the dark and snakes, if the Father says, "Take this bucket and go milk the cow," don't hesitate. Go milk the cow. It's always worth it.

My Last Big Game

IT WAS MY one big chance in the last big game of the season to show them what I could do. But I made a knee-jerk decision, and it cost me dearly. We all know that another name for a knee-jerk decision is *disaster*. If you are like me, you've had a few of those disasters because you did not take time to pause and think through your options and goals before making that all-important decision.

That's exactly what happened to me during a Little League football game I'll never forget. Because I was not a good player, I hardly ever was called from the bench to the field. At ten years old, I was the youngest player on the team. To make matters worse, I was too skinny, too shy, and too afraid of getting hurt. I really did not want to play football, but all my friends played. That was real peer pressure in those days. With my attitude and my size, I didn't have the makings of a good football player.

But there was that one time when the coach sent me in for the last few minutes of a big game. We were already losing, so the coach didn't have much to lose by sending me in. Even though I was skinny and shy, I was fast. Maybe he felt sorry that I had just warmed the bench the whole season, or maybe he thought I could catch a long pass and outrun the other team. After all, I had caught some long passes a few times in practice.

No matter his reasoning, in I went.

The quarterback made a quick pass to me. To my own astonishment, I caught it. I actually had the football in my hands. Immediately, three gorillas smashed into me from three sides. When I quit spinning and opened my eyes, I could hardly believe I was still standing and still breathing. So, with all that was in me, I took off running toward the goal post. I heard the crowd screaming. My adrenalin was pumping, and my emotions were soaring. I was about to make my first touchdown.

I crossed the goal line and waited for the crowd to cheer, but the crowd stopped yelling. I was puzzled. With all the screaming and getting knocked around, I didn't realize I had run full steam in the wrong direction and scored for the other team.

Over the years, there have been many times when I've gone back over that day in my mind, and I'll admit my face would turn a bit red. It was a defining moment that taught me two lessons I will always remember. First, too often life is like that football game. When something unexpected happens to knock me off balance and I am moving too fast, I usually don't take time to pause and make sure I am headed in the right direction. I don't usually stop and ask the Lord in what direction He wants me to go. It seems I have spent a good part of my life making knee-jerk, self-determined choices rather than wise, what-is-God's-will decisions.

One of my favorite writers and thinkers is Viktor

Frankl, the holocaust survivor and psychiatrist who learned how to make wise decisions through what he experienced during his time as a prisoner in the Auschwitz concentration camp. In his famous book *Man's Search for Meaning*, Frankl makes a profound observation: "Between stimulus and response there is a space. In that space is our power to choose our response. In our response lies our growth and our freedom."

Frankl learned the hard way what we all need to learn. It is in that brief time between what is happening to us and how we respond that we get to make a choice. We deliberately choose our response, or we just react to what is happening to us. What happens in that space is critical, for it determines whether we are making a wise, godly choice or a self-centered knee-jerk reaction. If we don't pause, we will surely make our own choice without God's leadership. That kind of choice will often make all the difference between a good and bad outcome in our attitudes, relationships, careers, finances, and so much more.

The Bible teaches that if we want to be wise in our Father's eyes and make the best choices, we will pause before every important decision to discover His will. That's what our Lord Jesus did. When faced with the reality of His crucifixion, Jesus could have chosen not to make that sacrifice. But He paused before making His decision. He got away from the crowd. He found a quiet space to stop and talk to His Father. His words and heart should be our words and heart: "Father, if you are willing, please take this cup of suffering away from me.

Yet I want your will to be done, not mine" (Luke 22:42 NLT).

Not only when facing the cross, but before all of Jesus' decisions, He first paused to find His Father's will. Jesus said, "I can do nothing on my own. I judge as God tells me. Therefore, my judgment is just, because I carry out the will of the one who sent me, not my own will" (John 5:30 NLT).

Looking back in the Old Testament to the early part of Solomon's life, God called him the wisest man in the world. What was Solomon's way of making decisions? He said, "Trust in the Lord with all your heart; do not depend on your own understanding. Seek his will in all you do, and he will show you which path to take" (Proverbs 3:5–6 NLT).

Simply put, my defining moment taught me that trusting in the Lord and continually admitting I need His help is the way to find true wisdom. Wisdom is trusting, waiting, pausing, giving time, making space for His Spirit to speak to us so that we are not depending on our own abilities, but we are wisely depending on Him to guide us to make important decisions.

I learned a second unforgettable lesson in that gridiron catastrophe. When that embarrassing game ended, my father ran up to me and put his arms around me and said, "Don't worry about it, son. Everyone makes mistakes. There'll be another day, another game. You gave it your best, and I'm proud of how you did."

Daddy witnessed the whole thing and loved me anyway. Daddy believed in me and stood up for me even though I went the wrong way. What Daddy thought about me meant more to me than what everyone else thought.

That's what our heavenly Father does over and over. He loves us and stands with us even though we too often go the wrong direction. That one defining moment gave me two principles to live by: pause and look for God's direction, and work not to please others but do the will of God as best I understand it and work to please Him. How grateful I am for God's guidance, His understanding, and His unconditional love.

Phyllis Clark Nichols

A NATIVE OF Cairo, Georgia, Phyllis did her undergraduate work at Valdosta State University and went on to receive her master of music degree from Southwestern Baptist Theological Seminary in Fort Worth, TX. Using her musical training, she has been a church pianist, a recording artist, and a concert artist for state conventions, conferences, civic groups, and local churches.

Phyllis was a cofounder and chief operating officer of a national health and wellness television and Internet program distribution service.

A retiree from the cable television industry, Phyllis now spends her time writing. Her character-driven southern fiction explores profound human questions using the imagined residents of smalltown communities you just know you've visited before. Her novels include the Rockwater Suite, a series of five books, and the three-book Family Portrait Series. She has also written two Christmas books: *Silent Days, Holy Night* and *Christmas at Grey Sage.* Phyllis is a Selah Award finalist for her nonfiction work *Sacred Sense from Taking a Second Look* and an International Book Awards Finalist for *Searching for the Song,* Book 5 in her Rockwater Suite.

With a strong faith and a love for nature, art, music, travel, and ordinary people, she tells redemptive tales of loss and recovery, estrangement and connection, longing, and fulfillment...often through surprisingly serendipitous events.

Phyllis currently serves on a number of nonprofit boards. She is mom to two daughters, and nana to three grandchildren. She lives in the Texas Hill Country with her portrait-artist, theologian husband, Dr. Bill Nichols.

Website: PhyllisClarkNichols.com
Facebook: facebook.com/Phyllis Clark Nichols
Twitter: twitter.com/PhyllisCNichols

Doors and Book Covers

GOD CAN AND often leads us through many doors and experiences to teach us about ourselves and our relationship to Him and others. Sometimes those doors are metaphorical, but at other times they are solid wooden doors like the one God opened for me when I was sixteen.

As a child, I was labeled the petite, puny girl with asthma who couldn't run or throw a ball or play outside, but I was never lonely or bored. I found the piano, and I discovered I could travel to magical places and meet such interesting people with a book in my hands. So, I opened the covers and read biographies and novels. I stepped into worlds that were foreign and others that were familiar. I felt as though I had lived on the moors of England, on the rocky coasts of Ireland, and near the blue topaz waters of Greece—all that between the covers of a book. I have felt the angst, the joys, the sorrows, the hope, and the hopelessness of captivating characters. I have even found new ways of thinking about something as old as time.

A book cover is just an open door to new experiences, but it was a real door that God led me through to experience a defining moment in my life.

Let me tell you how I came to that door. My senior year in high school was an especially arduous trip through Virgil's *Aeneid.* I was the one student who wanted a third year of Latin, and my devoted teacher agreed to guide my independent study that year. She assigned me to translate the first six books of the *Aeneid,* over four thousand lines of classical Latin dactylic hexameter with special attention to Book Six. That is where Aeneas journeyed into hell with me right behind him, translating every word.

In our school, we had the senior term paper—that dreaded thing students started talking about in the ninth grade, knowing we'd be held hostage without a high-school diploma if we did not write it. My Latin and English teachers conspired and assigned my term paper topic: "A Comparative Study of Dante's *Inferno* with Aeneas's Descent into Hell in the Sixth Book of the *Aeneid.*" The assignment was onerous, but it opened the world of research to me. And it also opened a door that became a defining moment.

The small, South Georgia town where I grew up was surrounded by plantations, soft rolling pine forests with fern-covered floors, and lazy creeks. And one of those plantations was owned by a gentleman who happened to be a world-renowned Dante scholar. How serendipitous (or so I thought at the time)! I discovered his work in my research and immediately decided I should meet this gentleman, Thomas C. Chubb. With my dad's help and introduction, I wrote to Mr. Chubb, and he was kind enough to grant me a meeting.

On a frigid, rainy Saturday morning in January, he opened his door, his library, and his world to me. His library was wall-to-wall, floor-to-ceiling mahogany bookshelves with a fireplace and large windows framed with heavy drapes. Books and journals were scattered across his desk and chairside tables. The room was like nothing I had ever seen before, and so was he. He was a handsome, distinguished-looking older gentleman in his smoking jacket and ascot, with a pipe that smelled so good it made me want to smoke. It was like a scene in so many of those English novels I had read—even down to being served tea by a uniformed lady late morning. Mr. Chubb and I spent two hours talking Dante and Virgil and the power and the beauty of the story.

Mr. Chubb was welcoming and willing to answer my sixteen-year-old questions patiently and to steer me into further research. His request for a copy of my finished paper and then his encouraging note after reading it were beyond thrilling to me. For years, I kept that term paper and his handwritten note. Unfortunately, they went the way of most things stored in the family attic after decades.

Before the doors to his library and his plantation home closed behind me, I now wish I had turned to tell him how walking into his world on that icy morning in January of 1969 changed my world. He never knew the impact those two hours spent with him had on my life. That was the defining moment when I truly understood how important books and stories were and that more than anything else as my vocation, I wanted to write.

And then life happened. Education and career and family responsibilities became my focus, but I never lost my desire to write. All along, I found avenues allowing me to be creative with words. I kept opening books, reading other people's stories, and realizing how important the story is for understanding life and human nature. Forty-six years later, when I had lived, loved, and suffered enough to have stories to write, my first novel was published with ten more to follow.

What is said about hindsight is accurate: it is always clearer. In looking back at that defining moment, I realize there were important lessons for me in that experience. The first is that none of my experience was simply a serendipity or good luck. God was at work shaping me for the purpose for which He designed me. It was my childhood sickliness that led me to books. Then, at just the right time, God provided a marvelous teacher to foster my fascination with language. I realized my meeting with Mr. Chubb was a gift God orchestrated—a gift that opened the world of writing and research to me.

Another lesson I learned was the power and influence of one's time and encouragement on another life. Mr. Chubb just happened to be the character in that defining moment, but there were many others who invested in me, leading me to be prepared for that moment. There were my parents, teachers, Sunday school teachers, and others who influenced my life as they shared their knowledge, wisdom, and their own life stories with me. Sometimes we get to see the value of our investment in another, but more often we do not. We may never know until we get to heaven, but because we do not know, it does not lessen the importance of giving of ourselves to others.

Often, I have regretted that Mr. Chubb never knew the impact he had on my life. Oh, I wrote a personal note of gratitude for his time on that January morning, but I never took the opportunity to let him know how that morning influenced my life and work. By the time I realized the importance of telling him, it was too late. That is the last the lesson I learned from my defining moment: we must let others know how they have positively influenced our lives while we can.

The doors that God opens for us and the doors we open for others can be life-defining moments. Never hesitate to enter, and never close them without saying, "Thank you."

Living in the Present

FOR SO MANY years in my work life, planning was a big part of my responsibility. My organizer, filled with assignments, action plans, projections, and lists, was hardly ever more than an arm's length away, always there to keep me on track. Oh, the lists! And the meetings! And the travel! When I retired, I planned to have a ceremony and burn that organizer. Without being tethered to it, I'd be free of the bondage of list making and endless appointments.

For so long it seemed that I had lived in the anticipation of what was coming—the next big event, the next year-end report, the next vacation, something on the horizon that would be better or perhaps worse. Sometimes that anticipation was exciting, and other times it brought dread.

Nevertheless, retirement brought a change of pace, and I was searching for something that I couldn't quite define. Maybe it was spontaneity.

Not to be. It turns out that spontaneity was not something I could pull off. I had lived too many years with structure and needed it still. So, my organizer sat looming quietly, staring at me from the table beside my favorite chair. Occasionally I opened it and made notes as I received invitations to do something of value with my time, things that were good for others and for God's Kingdom.

My early-morning practice was to sit in my cuddle chair in the studio for my quiet time after breakfast. This particular morning, I was comfortable with my cup of tea and the lovely view of the garden through the studio windows. As I read my Bible, these words from the book of James almost leaped off the page. "How do you know what your life will be like tomorrow? Your life is like the morning fog—it's here a little while, then it's gone" (James 4:14 NLT).

That was a sobering, mind-jostling thought. God has His way of choosing moments to speak, and this was my moment in my struggle. God's voice was not audible, but those words and this revelation came to me like a trumpet fanfare. I read them over and over, letting them sink into my being one by one. Realizing that my life on this earth is short—just a mist or vapor that will soon disappear—gave me a new perspective on the present and the future.

As I meditated, I grieved over the present moments I had missed through the years while I was waiting on the next big event or working through my endless lists. I prayed, asking God to forgive me for not enjoying and appreciating all those present moments that had been gifts from Him all along. I asked Him to help me to learn to live in the present.

God answered my prayer, although His answer wasn't as sudden as the impact of the verse from James on that spring morning. Over time, I learned the balance of living in the present and for planning and putting things on my calendar. I looked to God for help in how to spend my time, determined not to allow others to fill my calendar with things to do and places to be. I confess that still I struggled with guilt when I said "No, thank you, I am committed to something else."

Over the next few months after that morning moment, I found myself more mindful and more fully present, whether I was in conversation with someone or taking a walk or chopping vegetables for a pot of soup. I became more relaxed. I became a better listener. But the most life-changing lesson was that I truly became mindful of God's presence and His activity in my life. I began to experience Him in the ordinary activities of my days. I had always known that He was present, but somehow I knew it differently now.

In realizing God's continual presence with me, I became a much more grateful person than I had ever been. The unrecognized myriad of blessings from before became my new list of things to thank God for every morning. But even more, I learned to speak my gratitude at the very moment I became mindful of something for which I was grateful. The simplest of life's pleasures became my greatest delights. I found that when I focused on the many things for which I was grateful, I had no time for grumbling or complaining. Joy became the greatest by-product of my expressions of gratitude.

On that spring morning in the studio, God knew what was ahead of me, and He knew that I would need an awareness of His presence as my dear husband was diagnosed with three different cancers over the next few years. During those years, there were some difficult days, but I can honestly tell you there was always reason to be grateful because my Lord was present. And experiencing His presence brought peace and joy even on the darkest days.

Brother David Steindl-Rast says, "The root of joy is gratefulness. It is not joy that makes us grateful. It is gratitude that makes us joyful." Truly living in the present and being mindful of God's activity in my life and in His world have given me rest and a joy I never knew all because of a morning moment reading a verse in the book of James.

Made in the USA
Columbia, SC
04 July 2022